Federal Benefits for Veterans and Dependents

Second Edition

D1281671

A complete reprint of the U.S. Department of Veterans Affairs publication, *Federal Benefits for Veterans and Dependents,* 2002 Edition, with added sections based on information from the Office of Personnel Management, the Veterans Benefits Administration, and the Department of Veterans Affairs.

Special Discount for Veterans' Programs

As a way of saying thanks to our veterans, programs serving veterans (and their families) of the armed forces can purchase this book in full-case quantities at a 50 percent discount from retail price, plus shipping. To place an order or for additional information, please call toll-free 1-800-648-5478 and ask for a JIST sales staff member—or visit www.jist.com.

Your Domain
PUBLISHING

Federal Benefits for Veterans and Dependents, Second Edition

© 2003 by Your Domain Publishing

Published by Your Domain Publishing, an imprint of
JIST Publishing, Inc.
8902 Otis Avenue
Indianapolis, IN 46216-1033

Phone: 1-800-648-JIST   Fax: 1-800-JIST-FAX
E-mail: info@jist.com   Web site: www.jist.com

> **About career and life materials published by JIST.** Our materials encourage people to be self-directed and to take control of their destinies. We work hard to provide excellent content, solid advice, and techniques that get results. If you have questions about this book or other JIST products, call 1-800-648-JIST or visit www.jist.com.
>
> **Visit www.jist.com.** Find out about our products, get free book chapters, order a catalog, and link to other career-related sites. You can also learn more about JIST authors and JIST training available to professionals.

Printed in the United States of America
07 06 05 04 03 02   9 8 7 6 5 4 3 2 1

Credits and Acknowledgments

This book contains the complete reprint of the U.S. Department of Veterans Affairs publication, supplemented by bonus sections based on information from the Office of Personnel Management and the Veterans Affairs Web site.

We have been careful to provide accurate information throughout this book, but it is possible that errors and omissions have been introduced. Please consider this in making any career plans or other important decisions. Trust your own judgment above all else and in all things.

ISBN 1-930780-06-0

About This Book

Many veterans and their dependents qualify for benefits but don't know it. This book describes the numerous federal benefits available to veterans, their dependents, and their survivors; and it gives information on eligibility, completing applications, and filing claims.

JIST's enhanced version of *Federal Benefits for Veterans and Dependents,* 2002 Edition, includes the full text of the original Department of Veterans Affairs publication, plus informative bonus sections about the federal government's hiring preferences for veterans and reference materials for locating VA forms, facts, and answers online.

New information in this edition includes

- Expanded transition assistance and employment information
- World Wide Web links for fast access to VA offices and necessary forms
- Assistance for vets forming or expanding their own businesses
- Information about VONAPP, the VA's new online benefits application system

About Your Domain Publishing

Your Domain Publishing, an imprint of JIST Publishing, Inc., is committed to producing value-added government resources and providing greater access to the wealth of public domain information that is available.

We hope you find this high-quality reprint a handy resource, and that the bonus sections are especially useful. Please feel free to contact us at info@jist.com with any comments or questions.

Contents

Introduction

This pamphlet describes the variety of federal benefits available to veterans and their dependents. It contains information on benefits and programs that is accurate as of Jan. 1, 2002. Changes may occur during the year as a result of legislative or other requirements. The Department of Veterans Affairs (VA) World Wide Web pages are updated throughout the year to present the most current information. The VA home page (http://www.va.gov) contains links to sections on compensation and pension benefits, health-care benefits and services, burial and memorial benefits, home loan guarantees and other information of interest to veterans and their dependents.

Eligibility depends upon individual circumstances. Contact the nearest VA benefits office at 1-800-827-1000 from any location in the United States to apply. Counselors can answer questions about benefits eligibility and application procedures. They also make referrals to other VA facilities, such as medical centers and national cemeteries. Phone numbers of VA offices, including those in the Philippines and Puerto Rico, are listed in the back of this book. VA facilities also are listed in the federal government section of telephone directories under Department of Veterans Affairs.

Eligibility for most VA benefits is based upon discharge from active military service under other than dishonorable conditions. Active service means full-time service as a member of the Army, Navy, Air Force, Marine Corps, Coast Guard, or as a commissioned officer of the Public Health Service, the Environmental Services Administration or the National Oceanic and Atmospheric Administration. Current and former members of the Selected Reserve may be eligible for certain benefits, such as home loan guarantees and education, if they meet time-in-service and other criteria. Men and women veterans with similar service are entitled to the same VA benefits.

Service in 30 organizations during special periods that include World Wars I and II has been certified as active military service by the Department of Defense (DoD). Members of these groups, listed under "Special Groups" on the next page, may be eligible for VA benefits if DoD certifies their service and issues a discharge under other than dishonorable conditions. Members of a National Guard or reserve component ordered to active duty by order of the President may also be eligible to receive benefits.

Honorable and general discharges qualify a veteran for most VA benefits. Dishonorable and bad conduct discharges issued by general courts-martial bar VA benefits. Veterans in prison and parolees may be eligible for certain VA benefits. VA regional offices can clarify the eligibility of prisoners, parolees and individuals with multiple discharges issued under differing conditions.

Wartime Service: Certain VA benefits require wartime service. Under the law, VA recognizes these war periods:

Mexican Border Period: May 9, 1916, through April 5, 1917, for veterans who served in Mexico, on its borders or in adjacent waters.

World War I: April 6, 1917, through Nov. 11, 1918; for veterans who served in Russia, April 6, 1917, through April 1, 1920; extended through July 1, 1921, for veterans who had at least one day of service between April 6, 1917, and Nov. 11, 1918.

World War II: Dec. 7, 1941, through Dec. 31, 1946.

Korean War: June 27, 1950, through Jan. 31, 1955.

Vietnam War: Aug. 5, 1964 (Feb. 28, 1961, for veterans who served "in country" before Aug. 5, 1964), through May 7, 1975.

Gulf War: Aug. 2, 1990, through a date to be set by law or Presidential Proclamation.

Special Groups: A number of groups who have provided military-related service to the United States have been granted VA benefits. For the service to qualify, the Secretary of Defense must certify that the group has provided active military service. Individuals must be issued a discharge by the Secretary of Defense to qualify for VA benefits. Service in the following groups has been certified as active military service for benefits purposes:

1. Women Airforce Service Pilots (WASPs).
2. World War I Signal Corps Female Telephone Operators Unit.
3. Engineer Field Clerks.
4. Women's Army Auxiliary Corps (WAAC).
5. Quartermaster Corps female clerical employees serving with the American Expeditionary Forces in World War I.
6. Civilian employees of Pacific naval air bases who actively participated in defense of Wake Island during World War II.

7. Reconstruction aides and dietitians in World War I.

8. Male civilian ferry pilots.

9. Wake Island defenders from Guam.

10. Civilian personnel assigned to OSS secret intelligence.

11. Guam Combat Patrol.

12. Quartermaster Corps members of the Keswick crew on Corregidor during World War II.

13. U.S. civilians who participated in the defense of Bataan.

14. U.S. merchant seamen who served on blockships in support of Operation Mulberry in the World War II invasion of Normandy.

15. American merchant marines in oceangoing service during World War II.

16. Civilian Navy IFF radar technicians who served in combat areas of the Pacific during World War II.

17. U.S. civilians of the American Field Service who served overseas in World War I.

18. U.S. civilians of the American Field Service who served overseas under U.S. armies and U.S. army groups in World War II.

19. U.S. civilian employees of American Airlines who served overseas in a contract with the Air Transport Command between Dec. 14, 1941, and Aug. 14, 1945.

20. Civilian crewmen of U.S. Coast and Geodetic Survey vessels who served in areas of immediate military hazard while conducting cooperative operations with and for the U.S. Armed Forces between Dec. 7, 1941, and Aug. 15, 1945.

21. Members of the American Volunteer Group (Flying Tigers) who served between Dec. 7, 1941, and July 18, 1942.

22. U.S. civilian flight crew and aviation ground support employees of United Air Lines who served overseas in a contract with Air Transport Command between Dec. 14, 1941, and Aug. 14, 1945.

23. U.S. civilian flight crew and aviation ground support employees of Transcontinental and Western Air, Inc. (TWA), who served overseas in a contract with the Air Transport Command between Dec. 14, 1941, and Aug. 14, 1945.

24. U.S. civilian flight crew and aviation ground support employees of Consolidated Vultee Aircraft Corp. (Consairway Division) who served overseas in a contract with Air Transport Command between Dec. 14, 1941, and Aug. 14, 1945.

25. U.S. civilian flight crew and aviation ground support employees of Pan American World Airways and its subsidiaries and affiliates, who served overseas in a contract with the Air Transport Command and Naval Air Transport Service between Dec. 14, 1941, and Aug. 14, 1945.

26. Honorably discharged members of the American Volunteer Guard, Eritrea Service Command, between June 21, 1942, and March 31, 1943.

27. U.S. civilian flight crew and aviation ground support employees of Northwest Airlines who served overseas under the airline's contract with Air Transport Command from Dec. 14, 1941, through Aug. 14, 1945.

28. U.S. civilian female employees of the U.S. Army Nurse Corps who served in the defense of Bataan and Corregidor during the period Jan. 2, 1942, to Feb. 3, 1945.

29. U.S. flight crew and aviation ground support employees of Northeast Airlines Atlantic Division, who served overseas as a result of Northeast Airlines' contract with the Air Transport Command during the period Dec. 7, 1941, through Aug. 14, 1945.

30. U.S. civilian flight crew and aviation ground support employees of Braniff Airways, who served overseas in the North Atlantic or under the jurisdiction of the North Atlantic Wing, Air Transport Command, as a result of a contract with the Air Transport Command during the period Feb. 26, 1942, through Aug. 14, 1945.

Filipino Veterans:
Service-connected Commonwealth Army of the Philippines veterans and Filipino veterans with service during World War II in certain organized guerrilla forces who reside in the United States and are U.S. citizens or aliens lawfully admitted for permanent residence in the United States are eligible for hospital and nursing-home care and medical services in the same manner as U.S. veterans. Filipino veterans who served in the New Philippine Scouts and were discharged or released under conditions other than dishonorable are eligible for care in a VA health-care facility for the treatment of service-connected disabilities.

Health Care Enrollment: For most veterans, entry into the VA health-care system starts with applying for enrollment at a VA health-care facility. However, veterans with Internet access may apply for enrollment online (http://www.va.gov/1010ez.htm) by completing VA Form 10-10EZ, Application for Health Benefits. Once enrolled, a veteran is eligible to receive services at VA facilities anywhere in the country. Details of the enrollment program are discussed in the Health Care Benefits section of this publication. VA health-care facilities also provide information on medical care, including readjustment counseling, and examinations for Agent Orange, radiation exposure and ailments incurred from service in the Gulf War. Additional information on enrollment, including enrollment forms and online applications, can be found on the World Wide Web (http://www.va.gov/health/elig/).

Filing VA Claims: Those seeking a VA benefit for the first time must submit a copy of their service discharge form (DD-214, DD-215, or for WWII veterans, a WD form), which documents service dates and type of discharge, or give their full name, military service number, branch and dates of service. The claim number assigned by VA to the initial claim should be referred to in subsequent correspondence.

Important Documents: The veteran's service discharge form should be kept in a safe location accessible to the veteran and next of kin or designated representative. The veteran's preference regarding burial in a national cemetery and use of a headstone provided by VA should be documented and kept with this information. The following documents will be needed for claims processing related to a veteran's death: (1) veteran's marriage certificate for claims of a surviving spouse or children; (2) veteran's death certificate if the veteran did not die in a VA health-care facility; (3) children's birth certificates or adoption papers to determine children's benefits; (4) veteran's birth certificate to determine parents' benefits.

Privacy Act: The Privacy Act affords individuals the right to access and request amendment of information collected and used by the federal government. For more information, contact the Privacy Act officer at the facility where the information is maintained or visit the Privacy and Security section on VA's home page (http://www.va.gov).

Información Para Veteranos De Habla Hispana y Sus Dependientes

La versión en español de este folleto se encuentra disponible en formato Adobe Acrobat a través de el link (http://www.va.gov/opa/feature/index.htm) en la página de la Oficina de Asuntos Públicos del Departamento de Asuntos de Veteranos (VA) en la red mundial del internet. Las oficinas del VA en areas de gran concentración de veteranos y dependientes hispanos tienen disponibles consejeros bilingües que le pueden ayudar a aplicar para obtener beneficios. Puede encotrar una lista de las oficinas del VA en la parte de atrás de este folleto.

Health Care Benefits

Health Care Enrollment

To receive health care, veterans generally must be enrolled with VA. They may apply for enrollment at any time. Veterans living or traveling overseas must register with the Foreign Medical Program regardless of the degree of disability. See the Overseas Benefits section for more information. Veterans do not have to be enrolled if they: (1) have a service-connected disability of 50 percent or more; (2) want care for a disability that the military determined was incurred or aggravated in the line of duty, but which VA has not yet rated, during the 12-month period following discharge; or (3) want care for a service-connected disability only. To permit better planning of health resources, however, these three categories of veterans also are urged to enroll.

Veterans will be enrolled to the extent Congressional appropriations allow. If appropriations are limited, enrollment will occur based on the following priorities:

1. veterans with service-connected disabilities who are rated 50 percent or more disabled;

2. veterans with service-connected disabilities who are rated 30 or 40 percent disabled;

3. veterans who are former POWs or were awarded a Purple Heart, veterans with disabilities rated 10 and 20 percent, and veterans awarded special eligibility for disabilities incurred in treatment;

4. veterans who are receiving aid and attendance or housebound benefits and veterans who have been determined by VA to be catastrophically disabled;

5. veterans who are determined to be unable to defray the expenses of needed care;

6. all other eligible veterans who are not required to make copayments for their treatment. This includes veterans of the Mexican border period or of World War I; veterans seeking care solely for a disorder associated with exposure to a toxic substance or radiation, for a disorder associated with service in the Southwest Asia theater of operations during the Gulf War, or for any illness associated with service in combat in a war after the Gulf War or during a period of hostility after Nov. 11, 1998; and veterans with zero percent service-connected disabilities who are nevertheless compensated, including veterans receiving compensation for inactive tuberculosis.

7. Nonservice-connected veterans and noncompensable zero percent service-connected veterans who agree to pay copayments.

These groups are enrollment priorities only. The services and treatment available to enrolled veterans generally are not based on enrollment priority groups. Enrollment will be reviewed each year and veterans will be notified in writing of any change in their enrollment status. Call your nearest health-care facility or the Health Benefits Service Center, 1-877-222-8387, to obtain the latest information. Additional information on enrollment, including enrollment forms and online applications, also can be found on the World Wide Web (http://www.va.gov/health/elig/).

Financial Assessment

Veterans who want to enroll in priority group 5 based on their inability to defray the cost of their care must provide VA with information on their annual income and net worth to determine whether they are below the annually adjusted "means test" financial threshold. A veteran's household income is considered when making this means test assessment.

The "means test" eligibility assessment includes Social Security, U.S. Civil Service retirement, U.S. Railroad retirement, military retirement, unemployment insurance, any other retirement income, total wages from all employers, interest and dividends, workers' compensation, black lung benefits and any other gross income for the calendar year prior to application for care. Also considered are assets such as the market value of stocks, bonds, notes, individual retirement accounts, bank deposits, savings accounts and cash. The patient may fill out VA Form 10-10EZ at the time application for enrollment is made. VA forms can be found on the World Wide Web at the VA forms website (http://www.va.gov/forms/default.asp). VA may compare income information provided by the veteran with information obtained from the Social Security Administration and the Internal Revenue Service.

Services Requiring Copayments

A veteran who is not in priority group 1 through 6 whose income is above the "means test" threshold must agree to pay copayments for care. If the veteran does not agree to make copayments, the veteran will be ineligible for VA care. Patients whose income is determined to be above the means test threshold are responsible for the Medicare deductible for the first 90 days of care during any 365-day period. For each additional 90 days of hospital care, the patient is charged one-half the Medicare deductible. In addition to these charges, the patient is charged $10 a day for hospital care. With certain exceptions, a veteran must agree to pay copayments for the receipt of extended care services. A veteran's application for extended care services (VAF 10-10EC) requires financial information that is used to determine the monthly copayment amount, based on each individual veteran's financial situation. For outpatient care, a three-tiered copayment system is effective for all services provided on an outpatient basis. The copayment is $15 for a primary care visit and $50 for some outpatient visits, although there are some outpatient visits that do not result in a copayment.

Outpatient Visits Not Requiring Copayments

Outpatient visits for which no copayment will be assessed are: publicly announced VA public health initiatives (e.g., health fairs) or an outpatient visit solely consisting of preventive screening and/or immunizations, such as influenza immunization, pneumonococcal immunization, hypertension screening, hepatitis C screening, tobacco screening, alcohol screening, hyperlipidemia screening, breast cancer screening, cervical cancer screening, screening for colorectal cancer by fecal occult blood testing, and education about the risks and benefits of prostate cancer screening. Laboratory, flat film radiology services, and electrocardiograms are also exempt from copayments.

Billing Insurance Companies

VA is authorized to submit claims to health insurance carriers for recovery of VA's reasonable charges in providing medical care to nonservice-connected veterans and to service-connected veterans for nonservice-connected conditions. Money collected in this way is used to maintain and improve VA's health-care system for veterans. VA cannot bill Medicare for medical services provided to veterans.

All veterans applying for VA medical care will be asked to provide information on their health insurance coverage, including coverage provided under policies of their spouses. Although veterans are not responsible for paying any remaining balance of VA's insurance claim that is not paid or covered by their health insurance, veterans whose income is above the "means test" threshold are responsible for the VA copayments required by federal law. However, when VA receives payment from the veteran's health insurance company for the care furnished, VA credits that recovery toward the amount of the veteran's copayment obligation.

Nursing-Home Care

Nursing care in VA or private nursing homes may be provided for veterans who are not acutely ill and not in need of hospital care. VA will provide nursing-home care to veterans whose service-connected disability requires such care and to veterans with a service-connected disability rated at 70 percent or more who need this type of care. In addition, if space and resources are available, VA may also provide nursing-home care to other veterans.

Nonservice-connected veterans and zero percent, noncompensable, service-connected veterans requiring nursing-home care for any nonservice-connected disability must complete the financial section on VA Form 10-10EZ, to determine whether they will be billed for nursing-home care. To determine their copayment responsibility, certain veterans applying for nursing home care services will be required to provide additional income information on the VA Form 10-10EC, Application for Extended Care Benefits.

Some veterans may be eligible for VA nursing-home care without an income eligibility assessment, including veterans with a compensable, service-connected disability, those requiring nursing-home care for a disorder associated with exposure to a toxic substance or radiation, those requiring nursing-home care for a disorder associated with service in the Southwest Asia theater of operations during the Gulf War, veterans receiving treatment for sexual trauma and veterans receiving certain care or services for cancer of the head and neck. Also eligible are veterans with an illness associated with service in combat in a war after the Gulf War or during a period of hostility after Nov. 11, 1998.

Veterans who are receiving health care from VA may be transferred to a private nursing home at VA expense. This care normally may not be provided in excess of six months, except for veterans who need nursing-home care for a service-connected disability or veterans who were hospitalized primarily for treatment of a service-connected disability when funding is available and such care has been determined by a VA physician to be medically appropriate.

Domiciliary Care

Domiciliary care provides rehabilitative and long-term, health-maintenance care for veterans who require minimal medical care but who do not need the skilled nursing services provided in nursing homes. VA may provide domiciliary care to veterans whose annual income does not exceed the maximum annual rate of VA pension or to veterans the Secretary of Veterans Affairs determines have no adequate means of support. The copayments for extended care services apply to domiciliary care. Call your nearest benefits or health-care facility to obtain the latest information.

Outpatient Pharmacy Services

Outpatient pharmacy services are provided free to: (1) veterans with a service-connected disability of 50 percent or more; (2) veterans receiving medication for treatment of service-connected conditions; (3) veterans whose income does not exceed the maximum VA annual rate of the VA pension; (4) veterans receiving medication for conditions related to exposure to Agent Orange or ionizing radiation; (5) veterans receiving medication for conditions related to Gulf War or post-Gulf War service; (6) veterans receiving medication for conditions related to sexual trauma experienced while in the military; (7) veterans receiving medication for treatment of cancer of the head or neck and (8) veterans receiving medication as part of a VA-approved research project. Other veterans will be charged a copayment of $7 for each 30-day or less supply of medication. To eliminate a financial hardship for veterans who require an unusually large amount of medications, there is a maximum copayment amount that veterans enrolled in Priority Groups 2 through 6 pay in any single year. Priority groups are described on pages 6 and 7 of this booklet. Veterans do not pay copayments for medications dispensed during the remainder of a calendar year in which this annual cap amount has been paid. For calendar year 2002, the cap is $840.

The medication copayment applies to prescription and over-the-counter medications, such as aspirin, cough syrup or vitamins, dispensed by a VA pharmacy. Medication copayments are not charged for medications injected during the course of treatment or for medical supplies, such as syringes or alcohol wipes.

Outpatient Dental Treatment

Outpatient dental treatment provided by VA includes examinations and the full spectrum of diagnostic, surgical, restorative and preventive procedures. Some veterans receiving dental care may be billed the applicable copayment if their income exceeds the maximum threshold. The following veterans may receive care: (1) veterans having service-connected and compensable dental disabilities or conditions; (2) former prisoners of war imprisoned 90 days or more; (3) veterans with service-connected, noncompensable dental conditions as a result of combat wounds or service injuries; (4) veterans with nonservice-connected dental conditions determined by VA to be aggravating a medical problem; (5) veterans having service-connected conditions rated as total; and (6) veterans participating in a vocational rehabilitation program.

Veterans may receive one-time dental treatment for service-connected and noncompensable dental disabilities or conditions if the following conditions are met: the dental condition can be shown to have existed at time of discharge; the veteran served on active military duty for at least 180 days, (or 90 days during Gulf War Era); the veteran applied to VA for dental care within 90 days of discharge or release from active duty, and the certificate of discharge does not include certification that all appropriate dental treatment had been rendered prior to discharge.

Gulf War, Agent Orange and Ionizing Radiation Registry Programs

VA has developed databases called registries to help analyze the type of health conditions being reported by veterans who served in the Gulf War (Aug. 2, 1990 to a date not yet established), claim exposure to Agent Orange during the Vietnam War (between 1962 and 1975), served in Korea in 1968 or 1969, claim exposure to atomic radiation, or were treated with nasopharyngeal (NP) radium during military service. These veterans are provided with free, comprehensive medical examinations, including laboratory and other diagnostic tests deemed necessary by an examining physician to determine health status. Other veterans who may have been exposed to dioxin or other toxic substances in a herbicide or defoliant associated with the testing, transporting or spraying of herbicides for military purposes also are eligible to participate in the Agent Orange registry program.

Eligible veterans do not have to be enrolled in VA health care to participate in registry examinations. Examination results, along with reviews of veterans' military service and exposure histories, are entered into the registries. Participants are advised of the results of their examinations in personal consultations and by letters. Veterans wishing to participate should contact the nearest VA health-care facility for an examination.

Beneficiary Travel

Veterans may be eligible for payment or reimbursement for travel costs to receive VA medical care. Reimbursement is paid at $.11 per mile and is subject to a deductible of $3 for each one-way trip and an $18-per-month maximum payment. Two exceptions to the deductible are travel for a compensation or pension examination and travel by special modes of transportation, such as an ambulance or a specially equipped van. Beneficiary travel payments may be made to the following: (1) veterans whose service-connected disabilities are rated at 30 percent or more; (2) veterans traveling for treatment of a service-connected condition; (3) veterans who receive a VA pension; (4) veterans traveling for scheduled compensation or pension examinations; (5) veterans whose income does not exceed the maximum annual VA pension rate; and (6) veterans whose medical condition requires special mode of transportation, if the veteran is unable to defray the costs and travel is pre-authorized. Advance authorization is not required in a medical emergency if a delay would be hazardous to life or health.

Alcohol and Drug-Dependence Treatment

Veterans eligible for VA medical care may apply for substance abuse treatment. Contact the nearest VA medical facility to apply.

Home Improvements and Structural Alterations

The Home Improvements and Structural Alterations program provides funding for eligible veterans to make home improvements necessary for the continuation of treatment or for disability access to the home and essential lavatory and sanitary facilities. Home improvement benefits up to $4,100 for service-connected veterans and up to $1,200 for nonservice-connected veterans may be provided. For application information, contact the prosthetic representative at the nearest VA medical center or outpatient clinic.

Prosthetic and Sensory Aid Services

VA will furnish prosthetic appliances, equipment, and devices, such as artificial limbs, orthopedic braces and shoes, wheelchairs, crutches and canes, to veterans receiving VA care for any condition. VA will provide hearing aids and eyeglasses to veterans who receive increased pension based on the need for regular aid and attendance or being permanently housebound, receive compensation for a service-connected disability or are former prisoners of war. Otherwise, hearing aids and eyeglasses will be provided only in special circumstances, and not for generally occurring hearing or vision loss. For additional information, contact the prosthetic representative at your local VA health-care facility.

Services and Aids for Blind Veterans

Blind veterans may be eligible for services at a VA medical center or for admission to a VA blind rehabilitation center. Services are available at all VA medical facilities through the Visual Impairment Services coordinator. In addition, blind veterans entitled to receive disability compensation may receive VA aids for the blind.

Aids and services for blind veterans include:
1. a total health and benefits review by a VA Visual Impairment Services team;
2. adjustment to blindness training;
3. home improvements and structural alterations to homes;
4. specially adapted housing and adaptations;
5. low-vision aids and training in their use;
6. electronic and mechanical aids for the blind, including adaptive computers and computer-assisted devices such as reading machines and electronic travel aids;
7. guide dogs, including the expense of training the veteran to use the dog and the cost of the dog's medical care; and
8. talking books, tapes and Braille literature.

Readjustment Counseling

Readjustment counseling is provided at community-based Vet Centers to help veterans resolve psychological war trauma and to help them achieve a successful post-war adjustment to civilian life. Assistance includes group, individual and family counseling. Eligible veterans include those who served on active duty in a combat theater during World War II, the Korean War, the Vietnam War, the Gulf War, or the campaigns in Lebanon, Grenada, Panama, Somalia, Bosnia, Kosovo or Afghanistan. Veterans who served in the active military during the Vietnam Era, but not in the Republic of Vietnam, are also eligible, provided they request services at a Vet Center before Jan. 1, 2004.

Psychological readjustment problems include post traumatic stress disorder, or PTSD. This refers to such symptoms as nightmares, intrusive recollections or memories, anxiety or sudden reactions following exposure to traumatic wartime conditions. Readjustment difficulties may affect functioning in school, family or work.

Counseling also is provided for trauma due to sexual assault or harassment while on active duty. In areas distant from Vet Centers or VA medical facilities, veterans may obtain readjustment counseling from private-sector professionals who are on contract with VA. To obtain additional information about available services, contact the nearest Vet Center.

Medical Care for Dependents and Survivors

CHAMPVA, the Civilian Health and Medical Program of the Department of Veterans Affairs, provides reimbursement for most medical expenses – inpatient, outpatient, mental health, prescription medication, skilled nursing care, and durable medical equipment. To be eligible for CHAMPVA, an individual cannot be eligible for TRICARE (the medical program for civilian dependents provided by the Department of Defense formerly called CHAMPUS) and must be one of the following:

1. the spouse or child of a veteran who VA has rated as 100% permanently and totally disabled for a service-connected disability;
2. the surviving spouse or child of a veteran who died from a VA-rated service-connected disability, or who, at the time of death, was rated 100% permanently and totally disabled; or
3. the surviving spouse or child of a military member who died in the line of duty, not due to misconduct. In most of these cases, these family members are eligible for TRICARE, not CHAMPVA.

Individuals over the age of 65 must also meet additional CHAMPVA benefits eligibility conditions. Individuals who reached age 65 before June 5, 2001, and only have Medicare Part A, will be eligible for CHAMPVA without having to have Medicare Part B coverage; those who have Medicare Parts A and B, must keep both parts. Individuals who reached age 65 on or after June 5, 2001, must be enrolled in Medicare Parts A and B to be eligible.

For more information, or to apply for CHAMPVA benefits, visit the CHAMPVA Web site (http://www.va.gov/hac/), call 1-800-733-8387 or contact the VA Health Administration Center, P.O. Box 65023, Denver, CO 80206.

Many VA medical centers provide services to CHAMPVA beneficiaries under the CHAMPVA In House Treatment Initiative (CITI) program. CHAMPVA beneficiaries who use a CITI facility incur no cost for the services they receive. However, services provided under

14

this program are on a space available basis, after the needs of veterans are met. Because of this, not all services are available at all times, nor are the same services available every day. CHAMPVA beneficiaries should contact their nearest VA medical center to see if it is a participating facility.

Veterans Living or Traveling Overseas

VA will pay veterans living or traveling overseas for medical care associated with a service-connected condition. See the Overseas Benefits section for more information.

Merchant Marine Seamen

Merchant Marine seamen who served in World War II may qualify for veterans benefits. When applying for medical care, seamen must present their discharge certificate from the Department of Defense to the VA medical facility. VA regional offices can assist in obtaining a certificate.

Allied Veterans

VA is authorized to provide medical care to certain veterans of nations allied or associated with the United States during World War I or World War II. Such treatment is available at any VA medical facility if authorized and reimbursed by the foreign government. VA also is authorized to provide hospitalization, outpatient and domiciliary care to former members of the armed forces of Czechoslovakia or Poland who participated during World Wars I or II in armed conflict against an enemy of the United States, if they have been citizens of the United States for at least 10 years.

Emergency Medical Care in Non-VA Facilities

VA will provide reimbursement or payment for medical care provided to enrolled veterans by non-VA facilities only in cases of medical emergencies when (1) VA or other federal facilities were not feasibly available and (2) delay in seeking immediate medical attention would have been hazardous to the veteran's life or likely to result in serious harm. Other conditions also apply. To determine eligibility or to initiate a claim, contact the VA medical facility nearest to where the emergency service was provided.

Benefit Programs

Disability Compensation

Disability compensation is a monetary benefit paid to veterans who are disabled by injury or disease incurred or aggravated during active military service. The service of the veteran must have been terminated through separation or discharge under conditions that were other than dishonorable. Disability compensation varies with the degree of disability and the number of dependents, and is paid monthly. The benefits are not subject to federal or state income tax. The payment of military retirement pay, disability severance pay and separation incentive payments known as SSB and VSI (Special Separation Benefits and Voluntary Separation Incentives) also affects the amount of VA compensation paid. See the "Tables" section of this booklet for more information.

Receiving Benefit Payments

VA offers three methods for receiving benefit payments. Nearly 80 percent of veterans and beneficiaries receive their payments by direct deposit through an electronic fund transfer to their bank, savings and loan or credit union accounts. In some areas, benefit recipients who do not have an account at a financial institution may open a federally insured Electronic Transfer Account, which costs about $3 a month, provides a monthly statement and allows cash withdrawals. Recipients may also choose to receive benefits by check. To choose a payment method, veterans and beneficiaries should call VA's toll-free helpline at 1-877-838-2778, Monday through Friday, 7:30 a.m. - 4:00 p.m., Central Standard Time.

Prisoners of War

Former prisoners of war who were imprisoned for at least 30 days are presumed to be eligible for disability compensation if they become at least 10 percent disabled from diseases associated with POWs. These presumptive diseases are avitaminosis, beriberi heart disease, ischemic heart disease and conditions where the prisoner of war experienced localized edema during captivity, chronic dysentery, helminthiasis, malnutrition (including optic atrophy), pellagra and/or other nutritional deficiencies, psychosis, anxiety states, dysthymic disorder, depressive neurosis, post-traumatic osteoarthritis, irritable bowel syndrome, peptic ulcer disease, peripheral neuropathy, residuals of cold injury (including arthritis, neuropathy, and/or skin cancer at the site of the cold injury).

Agent Orange and Other Herbicides

Ten diseases are presumed by VA to be service-related for compensation purposes for veterans exposed to Agent Orange and other herbicides used in support of military operations in the Republic of Vietnam between Jan. 9, 1962, and May 7, 1975. The diseases presumed are chloracne or other acneform disease similar to chloracne, porphyria cutanea tarda, soft-tissue sarcoma (other than osteosarcoma, chondrosarcoma, Kaposi's sarcoma or mesothelioma), Hodgkin's disease, multiple myeloma, respiratory cancers (lung, bronchus, larynx, trachea), non-Hodgkin's lymphoma, prostate cancer, acute and subacute peripheral neuropathy and diabetes mellitus (Type 2 diabetes).

Veterans Exposed to Radiation

Veterans exposed to ionizing radiation while on active duty may be eligible for disability compensation if they have disabilities related to that exposure. To determine service-connection, factors considered include amount of radiation exposure, duration of exposure, elapsed time between exposure and onset of the disease, gender and family history, age at time of exposure, the extent to which a nonservice-related exposure could contribute to disease and the relative sensitivity of exposed tissue. Conditions presumed to be service-connected are all forms of leukemia (except for chronic lymphocytic leukemia); cancer of the thyroid, breast, pharynx, esophagus, stomach, small intestine, pancreas, bile ducts, gall bladder, salivary gland, urinary tract, bronchiolo-alveolar carcinoma, multiple myeloma, lymphomas (other than Hodgkin's disease), and primary liver cancer, (except if cirrhosis or hepatitis B is indicated).

Gulf War Veterans

Gulf War veterans who suffer from chronic disabilities resulting from undiagnosed illnesses, medically unexplained chronic multi-symptom illnesses (such as chronic fatigue syndrome, fibromyalgia, or irritable bowel syndrome) that are defined by a cluster of signs or symptoms, and any diagnosed illness that the Secretary of Veterans Affairs determines warrants a presumption of service-connection may receive disability compensation. The undiagnosed illnesses must have appeared either during active duty in the Southwest Asia Theater of Operations during the Gulf War or to a degree of at least ten percent at any time since then through Sept. 30, 2006.

The following symptoms are among the manifestations of an undiagnosed illness: fatigue, skin disorders, headache, muscle pain, joint pain, neurologic symptoms, neuropsychological symptoms, symptoms involving the respiratory system, sleep disturbances, gastrointestinal symptoms, cardiovascular symptoms, abnormal weight loss and menstrual disorders. A disability is considered chronic if it has existed for at least six months.

National Guardsmen

Members of the National Guard activated for federal service during a period of war or domestic emergency may be eligible for certain VA benefits, such as VA health care or compensation for injuries or conditions connected to that service. Activation for other than federal service does not qualify guardsmen for all VA benefits. Claims for VA benefits based on federal service filed by guardsmen should include a copy of the military orders, presidential proclamation or executive order that clearly demonstrates the federal nature of the service.

Allowances for Dependents

Veterans whose service-connected disabilities are rated at 30 percent or more are entitled to additional allowances for dependents. The additional amount is determined by the number of dependents and the degree of disability. A disabled veteran evaluated 30 percent or more is entitled to receive a special allowance for a spouse who is in need of the aid and attendance of another person.

Incarcerated Veterans

VA benefits are restricted if a veteran, surviving spouse, child or dependent parent is convicted of a felony and imprisoned for more than 60 days. The disability compensation paid to an incarcerated veteran is limited to the 10 percent disability rate. For a surviving spouse, child, dependent parent or veteran whose disability rating is 10 percent, the payment is at the 5 percent rate. Any amounts not paid may be apportioned to eligible dependents. Payments are not reduced for recipients participating in work-release programs, residing in halfway houses or under community control. Overpayments for failure to notify VA of a veteran's incarceration result in the loss of all financial benefits until the overpayment is recovered.

Specially Adapted Homes

Disabled veterans may be entitled to a grant from VA for a home specially adapted to their needs or for adaptations to a house.

$48,000 Grant: VA may approve a grant of not more than 50 percent of the cost of building, buying or remodeling adapted homes or paying indebtedness on those homes already acquired, up to a maximum of $48,000. Veterans must be entitled to compensation for permanent and total service-connected disability due to one of the following:

1. loss or loss of use of both lower extremities, such as to preclude locomotion without the aid of braces, crutches, canes or a wheelchair;

2. disability that includes (a) blindness in both eyes, having only light perception, plus (b) loss or loss of use of one lower extremity;

3. loss or loss of use of one lower extremity together with (a) residuals of organic disease or injury, or (b) the loss or loss of use of one upper extremity, which so affects the functions of balance or propulsion as to preclude locomotion without the use of braces, canes, crutches or a wheelchair.

$9,250 Grant: VA may approve a grant for the actual cost, up to a maximum of $9,250, for adaptations to a veteran's residence that are determined by VA to be reasonably necessary. The grant also may be used to help veterans acquire a residence that already has adaptations for the veteran's disability. Veterans must be entitled to compensation for permanent and total service-connected disability due to (1) blindness in both eyes with 5/200 visual acuity or less, or (2) anatomical loss or loss of use of both hands.

Supplemental Financing: Veterans with available loan guaranty entitlement may also obtain a guaranteed loan or a direct loan from VA to supplement the grant to acquire a specially adapted home.

Automobile Assistance

Veterans and service members qualify for this benefit if they have service-connected loss or permanent loss of use of one or both hands or feet, or permanent impairment of vision of both eyes to a certain degree. Veterans entitled to compensation for ankylosis (immobility) of one or both knees, or one or both hips, also qualify for adaptive equipment for an automobile. There is a one-time payment by VA of not more than $9,000 toward the purchase of an automobile or other conveyance. VA pays for adaptive equipment, and for repair, replacement, or reinstallation required because of disability, and for the safe operation of a vehicle purchased with VA assistance. To apply, contact a VA regional office (1-800-827-1000) or a VA medical center.

Clothing Allowance

Any veteran who is entitled to receive compensation for a service-connected disability for which he or she uses prosthetic or orthopedic appliances may receive an annual clothing allowance. The allowance also is available to any veteran whose service-connected skin condition requires prescribed medication that irreparably damages the veteran's outer garments. To apply, contact a VA regional office.

Pension

Veterans with low incomes who are permanently and totally disabled may be eligible for monetary support if they have 90 days or more of active military service, at least one day of which was during a period of war. The discharge from active duty must have been under conditions other than dishonorable. The permanent and total disability must be for reasons other than the veteran's own willful misconduct. Payments are made to qualified veterans to bring their total income, including other retirement or Social Security income, to a level set by Congress. Unreimbursed medical expenses may reduce countable income. Veterans of a period of war who are aged 65 or older and meet service and income requirements are also eligible to receive a pension, regardless of current physical condition.

Improved Pension

The Improved Pension program provides for the maximum annual rates listed in the "Tables" section of this booklet. The payment is reduced by the amount of the countable income of the veteran and the income of the spouse or dependent children. When a veteran without a spouse or a child is furnished nursing-home or domiciliary care by VA, the pension is reduced to an amount not to exceed $90 per month after three calendar months of care. The reduction may be delayed if nursing-home care is being continued for the primary purpose of providing the veteran with rehabilitation services.

Protected Pension Programs

Pensioners entitled to benefits as of Dec. 31, 1978, who do not elect to receive a pension under the Improved Pension program, continue to receive pension benefits at the rate they were entitled to receive on Dec. 31, 1978, as long as they remain permanently and totally disabled, do not lose a dependent, a dependent pensioner retains surviving spouse or child status, net worth limitations are not exceeded, and their incomes do not exceed the income limitation, adjusted annually.

Aid and Attendance or Housebound

A veteran who is a patient in a nursing home and determined by VA to be in need of the regular aid and attendance of another person, or a veteran who is permanently housebound, may be entitled to higher income limitations or additional benefits, depending on the type of pension received.

Medal of Honor Pension

VA administers pensions to holders of the Medal of Honor. In December 1998, Congress set the monthly pension at $600.

Incarcerated Veterans

A veteran may not receive VA pension benefits while incarcerated for more than 60 days. The veteran's dependents, however, may receive a portion of such benefits. Failure to notify VA of a veteran's incarceration will cause the loss of all financial benefits until any overpayment is recovered.

Education and Training

Additional information for school officials, veterans and dependents can be found on VA's Education Services Web page (http://www.gibill.va.gov) or by calling 1-888-GI-BILL-1 (1-888-442-4551).

Montgomery GI Bill (Active Duty)
Eligibility

The Montgomery GI Bill (Active Duty) provides a program of education benefits to honorable discharged veterans who entered active duty for the first time after June 30, 1985. Active duty includes certain full-time Reserve and National Guard duty performed after June 30, 1985. To receive the maximum benefit, a participant must serve on active duty for three continuous years. An individual also may qualify for the full benefit by initially serving 24 continuous months on active duty, followed by four years of Selected Reserve service, beginning within one year of release from active duty.

To participate in the Montgomery GI Bill (MGIB), service members have their military pay reduced by $100 a month for the first 12 months of active duty. This money is not refundable. The participant generally must have a high school diploma or an equivalency certificate before beginning training. Completing a minimum of 12 credit hours toward a college degree meets this requirement. Credits granted by colleges for life experiences may be used to meet this requirement. Individuals who serve a continuous period of at least three years of active duty, even though they were initially obligated to serve less, will be paid the maximum benefit. Benefits under this program generally end 10 years from the date of the veteran's last discharge or release from active duty, but some extenuating circumstances qualify for extensions. A veteran with a discharge upgraded by the military will have 10 years from the date of the upgrade.

Vietnam Era GI Bill Conversions and other MGIB Enrollment
Individuals who had remaining entitlement under the Vietnam Era GI Bill when that program ended on Dec. 31, 1989, and served on active duty between Oct. 19, 1984, and July 1, 1985, and continued to serve on active duty to July 1, 1988, or to July 1, 1987, followed by four years in the Selected Reserve, are eligible for MGIB benefits. Those who were not on active duty on October 19, 1984, but served three continuous years on active duty on or after July 1, 1985, or two years on active duty followed by four years in the Selected Reserve on or after July 1, 1985, and had remaining Vietnam Era GI Bill entitlement on Dec. 31, 1989, also are eligible for MGIB benefits. An individual who converts from the Vietnam Era GI Bill must have had a high school diploma or an equivalency certificate before Dec. 31, 1989. Completion of 12 credit hours toward a college degree meets this requirement.

Individuals who were participants under the Post-Vietnam Era Veterans' Educational Assistance Program (VEAP) on or before Oct. 9, 1996, who continued to serve on active duty through at least April 1, 2000, had until Oct. 21, 2001, to make an irrevocable election to receive MGIB benefits. These individuals must have completed the requirements of a secondary school diploma (or equivalency certificate) or successfully completed the equivalent of 12 semester hours in a program of education leading to a standard college degree before applying for benefits. Those who elected this conversion must have been discharged or released from active duty with an honorable discharge and had their basic pay reduced by or made a lump-sum payment of $2,700.

Certain other individuals who are involuntarily separated from active duty after Feb. 2, 1991, may receive MGIB benefits, but they must agree to have their basic pay reduced by $1,200. Additionally, individuals who voluntarily separated on or after Oct. 23, 1992, under the Voluntary Separation Incentive or the Special Separation Benefit programs may participate in the MGIB program if they agreed to have their basic pay reduced by $1,200.

Discharges and Separations

For the Montgomery GI Bill program, the discharge must be honorable. Discharges designated "under honorable conditions" and "general" do not establish eligibility. An honorable discharge for one of the following reasons may result in a reduction of the required length of active duty: (1) convenience of the government; (2) disability; (3) hardship; (4) a medical condition existing before service; (5) force reductions; (6) physical or mental conditions which prevent satisfactory performance of duty.

Education and Training Available

The following are available under the Montgomery GI Bill: (1) courses at colleges and universities leading to associate, bachelor or graduate degrees, and accredited independent study; (2) courses leading to a certificate or diploma from business, technical or vocational schools; (3) apprenticeship or on-the-job training programs for individuals not on active duty; (4) correspondence courses, under certain conditions; (5) flight training, if the veteran has a private pilot license and meets the medical requirements upon beginning the training program; (6) tutorial assistance benefits if the individual is enrolled in school halftime or more, and refresher, deficiency and similar training; (7) state-approved teacher certification programs; (8) preparatory courses necessary for admission to a college or graduate school; (9) licensing and certification tests approved by the Secretary of Veterans Affairs; and (10) "Top-Up" benefits to cover costs approved for Tuition Assistance from the military that Tuition Assistance alone does not cover.

Work-Study

Participants may be paid a work-study allowance if they train at the three-quarter or full-time rate. They may elect to be paid in advance a portion of the allowance equal to 40 percent of the total. Participants under the supervision of a VA employee may provide VA outreach services, prepare and process VA paperwork, and work at a VA medical facility or perform other VA approved activities. They may also help at national or state veterans' cemeteries in addition to assisting in outreach services furnished by State Approving Agencies, which are state organizations that review, evaluate and approve education and training programs for GI Bill participation.

Counseling

Educational and vocational counseling may be available for individuals who are eligible for VA educational assistance, who are on active duty and within 180 days of discharge or who have been discharged one year or less. VA will help individuals understand their educational and vocational needs, and plan an educational or vocational goal.

Payments

Veterans who served on active duty for three years or more, or two years active duty plus four years in the Selected Reserve or National Guard, will receive $800 a month in basic benefits for 36 months. Those who enlist and serve for less than three years will receive $650 a month. VA will pay an additional amount, commonly called a "kicker," if directed by the Department of Defense.

Additional information, updates, documents and forms that will aid school officials, veterans and dependents can be found on the Internet (http://www.gibill.va.gov) or by calling 1-888-GI-BILL-1 (1-888-442-4551).

Montgomery GI Bill (Selected Reserve)

Eligibility

The Montgomery GI Bill (Selected Reserve) provides education benefits to members of the reserve elements of the Army, Navy, Air Force, Marine Corps and Coast Guard, and to members of the Army National Guard and the Air National Guard. To be eligible for the program, a reservist must: (1) have a six-year obligation to serve in the Selected Reserve signed after June 30, 1985, or, if an officer, agree to serve six years in addition to the original obligation; (2) complete Initial Active Duty for Training (IADT); (3) have a high school diploma or equivalency certificate before applying for benefits; and (4) remain in good standing in a Selected Reserve unit.

Education and Training Available

Reservists may seek an undergraduate degree, go for graduate training, or take technical courses at colleges and universities. Flight training also is allowed. Those who have a six-year commitment beginning after Sept. 30, 1990, may take courses for a certificate or diploma from business, technical or vocational schools; cooperative training; apprenticeship or on-the-job training; correspondence courses; independent study programs; flight training; tutorial assistance; remedial, refresher and other training; and state-approved certification programs for training alternate teachers.

Period of Eligibility

If a reservist stays in the Selected Reserve, benefits generally end 10 years from the date the reservist became eligible for the program. VA may extend the 10-year period if the individual could not train due to a disability caused by Selected Reserve service. Benefits generally end upon separation from the Selected Reserve. However, if a reservist separates because of a disability, the individual may use the full 10 years. VA may also extend the 10-year period if the reservist was ordered to active duty.

Individuals separated from the Selected Reserve due to downsizing of the military between Oct. 1, 1991, and Sept. 30, 1999, have the full 10 years to use their benefits. If the 10-year period ends while the participant is attending school, VA will pay benefits until the end of the term. If the training is not on a term basis, payments may continue for 12 weeks.

Work-Study

Participants may be paid a work-study allowance if they train at the three-quarter or full-time rate. They may elect to be paid in advance a portion of the allowance equal to 40 percent of the total. Participants under the supervision of a VA employee may provide VA outreach services, prepare and process VA paperwork, and work at a VA medical facility or perform other VA approved activities. They may also help at national or state veterans' cemeteries in addition to assisting in outreach services furnished by State Approving Agencies. MGIB Selected Reserve participants may also perform activities relating to the administration of MGIB benefits at Department of Defense, Coast Guard, or National Guard facilities.

Counseling

Educational and vocational counseling may be available for individuals who are eligible for VA educational assistance; who are on active duty and within 180 days of discharge; or who have been discharged one year or less. VA will help these individuals understand their educational and vocational strengths and weaknesses and plan an educational or vocational goal.

Payments

The full-time rate is $272 a month for 36 months.

Veterans' Educational Assistance Program (VEAP)

Eligibility

Under VEAP, active duty personnel voluntarily participated in a plan for education or training in which their savings were administered and added to by the federal government. Service members were eligible to enroll in VEAP if they entered active duty for the first time after Dec. 31, 1976, and before July 1, 1985. Some contribution to VEAP must have been made prior to April 1, 1987. The maximum participant contribution is $2,700. While on active duty, participants may make a lump-sum contribution to the training fund.

A service member who participated in VEAP is eligible to receive benefits while on active duty if: (1) at least three months of contributions are available, except for high school or elementary school, in which case only one month of contributions is needed; and (2) the first active-duty commitment is completed. If the individual's first term is for more than six years, benefits may be available after six years. To attend an elementary or high school program, the individual must be in the last six months of the first enlistment.

A veteran who participated in VEAP is eligible to receive benefits if the discharge was under conditions other than dishonorable on or after Jan. 1, 1977, and served for a continuous period of 181 days or more, or was discharged for a service-connected disability.

Education eligibility may be established even though the required active duty is not completed if the veteran was discharged or released for a service-connected disability.

Education and Training Available

VEAP participants may pursue associate, bachelor or graduate degrees at colleges or universities. Courses leading to a certificate or diploma from business, technical or vocational schools may also be taken. Other opportunities may include apprenticeship or on-the-job training programs; cooperative courses; correspondence courses; tutorial assistance; refresher, deficiency and other training; and state-approved alternative teacher certification programs. VEAP participants may also pursue licensing and certification tests approved by the Secretary of Veterans Affairs.

Flight training also may be pursued, including solo flying hours up to the minimum required by the FAA for the rating or certification being pursued. Before beginning training, the veteran must have a private pilot license and continue to meet the medical requirements for a commercial license throughout the training program.

A participant may study abroad in programs leading to a college degree and in programs which offer, as part of the curriculum, nontraditional training away from school. A participant with a deficiency in a subject may receive tutorial assistance benefits if enrolled halftime or more.

Period of Eligibility
A veteran has 10 years from the date of last discharge or release from active duty to use VEAP benefits. This 10-year period can be extended by the amount of time the veteran could not train because of a disability or because of being held by a foreign government or power. The 10-year period may also be extended if the veteran re-enters active duty for 90 continuous days or more after becoming eligible. For periods of less than 90 days, the veteran may qualify for extensions under certain circumstances. The extension ends 10 years from the date of discharge or release from the later active duty period. A veteran with a discharge upgraded by the military will have 10 years from the date of the upgrade.

Work-Study
Participants may be paid a work-study allowance if they train at the three-quarter or full-time rate. They may elect to be paid 40 percent of the total allowance in advance. Participants under the supervision of a VA employee may provide VA outreach services, prepare and process VA paperwork, and work at a VA medical facility or perform other VA approved activities. They may also help at national or state veterans' cemeteries in addition to assisting in outreach services furnished by State Approving Agencies.

Counseling
Educational and vocational counseling may be available for veterans who are eligible for VA educational assistance, who are on active duty and within 180 days of discharge or who have been discharged one year or less. VA will help individuals understand their educational and vocational needs and plan an educational or vocational goal.

Payments
When the participant elects to use VEAP benefits, the Department of Defense will match the participant's contribution at the rate of $2 for

every $1 the individual put into the fund. The department also may make additional contributions to the fund in exchange for special duties performed by the participant.

Vocational Rehabilitation and Employment

Vocational Rehabilitation and Employment is an employment-oriented program that assists veterans with service-connected disabilities by offering them services and assistance to help them prepare for, find and keep suitable employment. Suitable employment is work that is within the veterans' physical, mental and emotional capabilities and matches their patterns of skills, abilities and interests. For veterans whose disabilities make employment unlikely, VA helps them attain as much daily living independence as possible.

Eligibility
A veteran must have a VA-established service-connected disability of at least 10 percent with a serious employment handicap or 20 percent with an employment handicap and be discharged or released from military service under other than dishonorable conditions. A service member pending medical separation from active duty may apply, but the disability rating must be at least 20 percent.

Services
Depending on an individual's needs, services provided by VA may include:
    1. an evaluation of the individual's abilities, skills and interests;
    2. assistance finding and maintaining suitable employment;
    3. vocational counseling and planning;
    4. training, such as on-the-job and work experience programs;
    5. training, such as certificate, two, or four-year college or technical programs;
    6. supportive rehabilitation services and additional counseling.

VA pays the cost of these services and pays a living allowance to veterans who participate in a training program.

Entitlement
Eligible veterans are evaluated to determine if they need vocational rehabilitation services to help overcome barriers to employment.

Period of a Rehabilitation Program
Generally, veterans must complete a vocational rehabilitation pro-

gram within 12 years from their separation from military service or within 12 years from the date VA notifies them that they have a compensable service-connected disability. Depending on the length of program needed, veterans may be provided up to 48 months of full-time services or their part-time equivalent. These limitations may be extended in certain circumstances.

Work Study
Participants may be paid a work-study allowance if they train at the three-quarter or full-time rate. They may elect to be paid in advance a portion of the allowance equal to 40 percent of the total. Participants under the supervision of a VA employee may provide VA outreach services, prepare and process VA paperwork, and work at a VA medical facility or perform other VA-approved activities.

Program for Unemployable Veterans
Veterans awarded 100 percent disability compensation based upon unemployability may still request an evaluation. If they are found eligible, they may participate in a vocational rehabilitation program and receive help in getting a job. A veteran who secures employment under the special program will continue to receive 100 percent disability compensation until the veteran has worked continuously for at least 12 months.

Home Loan Guaranties

VA loan guaranties are made to service members, veterans, reservists and unmarried surviving spouses for the purchase of homes, condominiums and manufactured homes and for refinancing loans. VA guarantees part of the total loan, permitting the purchaser to obtain a mortgage with a competitive interest rate, even without a down payment if the lender agrees. VA requires that a down payment be made for the purchase of a manufactured home. VA also requires a down payment for a home or condominium if the purchase price exceeds the reasonable value of the property or the loan has a graduated payment feature. With a VA guaranty, the lender is protected against loss up to the amount of the guaranty if the borrower fails to repay the loan. A VA loan guaranty can be used to:
1. buy a home;
2. buy a residential condominium;
3. build a home;
4. repair, alter or improve a home;
5. refinance an existing home loan;

6. buy a manufactured home with or without a lot;

7. buy and improve a manufactured home lot;

8. install a solar heating or cooling system or other weatherization improvements;

9. purchase and improve a home simultaneously with energy-efficient improvements;

10. refinance an existing VA loan to reduce the interest rate and make energy-efficient improvements;

11. refinance a manufactured home loan to acquire a lot.

Eligibility

Applicants must have a good credit rating, have an income sufficient to support mortgage payments, and agree to live in the property. To obtain a VA Certificate of Eligibility, complete VA Form 26-1880, Request for a Certificate of Eligibility for VA Home Loan Benefits, and mail it to one of the two VA Eligibility Centers (Winston-Salem and Los Angeles). In general, those veterans living in the Western part of the country mail their applications to the Los Angeles Eligibility Center, while those living in the Eastern part of the country mail applications to Winston-Salem. You can find more information on eligibility and addresses for the Centers by contacting your local VA office or by visiting VA's loan guaranty eligibility page (http://www.homeloans.va.gov/elig.htm) on the World Wide Web.

World War II: (1) active duty service after Sept. 15, 1940, and prior to July 26, 1947; (2) discharge under other than dishonorable conditions; and (3) at least 90 days service unless discharged early for a service-connected disability.

Post-World War II: (1) active duty service after July 25, 1947, and prior to June 27, 1950; (2) discharge under other than dishonorable conditions; and (3) 181 days continuous active duty unless discharged early for service-connected disability.

Korean War: (1) active duty after June 26, 1950, and prior to Feb. 1, 1955; (2) discharge under other than dishonorable conditions; and (3) at least 90 days total service, unless discharged early for a service-connected disability.

Post-Korean War: (1) active duty between Jan. 31, 1955, and Aug. 5, 1964; (2) discharge under conditions other than dishonorable; (3) 181 days continuous service, unless discharged early for service-connected disability.

Vietnam: (1) Active duty after Aug. 4, 1964, and prior to May 8, 1975; (2) discharge under conditions other than dishonorable; and (3) 90 days total service, unless discharged early for service-connected disability. For veterans who served in the Republic of Vietnam, the beginning date is Feb. 28, 1961.

Post-Vietnam: For veterans whose enlisted service began before Sept. 8, 1980, or whose service as an officer began before Oct. 17, 1981: (1) active duty for 181 continuous days, all of which occurred after May 7, 1975, and discharge under conditions other than dishonorable; or (2) early discharge for service-connected disability.

For veterans separated from enlisted service between Sept. 8, 1980, and Aug. 1, 1990, or service as an officer between Oct. 17, 1981, and Aug. 1, 1990: (1) completion of 24 months of continuous active duty or the full period — at least 181 days — for which the person was called or ordered to active duty, and discharge under conditions other than dishonorable; or (2) completion of at least 181 days of active duty with a hardship discharge or discharge for the convenience of the government, reduction-in-force or certain medical conditions; or (3) early discharge for service-connected disability.

Gulf War: (1) completion of 24 months of continuous active duty or the full period — at least 90 days — for which the person was called to active duty, and discharge from active duty under conditions other than dishonorable; or (2) discharge after at least 90 days with a hardship discharge, discharge at the convenience of the government, reduction-in-force or certain medical conditions, or discharge for service-connected disability. Reservists and National Guard members are eligible if they were activated after Aug. 1, 1990, served at least 90 days, and were discharged honorably.

Active Duty Personnel: Until the Gulf War era is ended by law or Presidential Proclamation, persons on active duty are eligible after serving on continuous active duty for 90 days.

Members of the Selected Reserve: Individuals are eligible if they have completed at least six years in the reserves or National Guard or were discharged because of a service-connected disability. This eligibility expires Sept. 30, 2009. Reservists who do not qualify for VA housing loan benefits may be eligible for loans on favorable terms insured by the Federal Housing Administration (FHA) of the Department of Housing and Urban Development (HUD).

Others: Other eligible individuals include unmarried spouses of veterans or reservists who died on active duty or as a result of service-connected causes; spouses of active-duty service members who have been missing in action or a prisoner of war for at least 90 days; U.S. citizens who served in the armed forces of a U.S. ally in World War II; and members of organizations with recognized contributions to the U.S. World War II effort. Eligibility may be determined at the VA Eligibility Centers.

Guaranty Amount

The amount of the VA guaranty available to an eligible veteran is called the entitlement and may be considered the equivalent of a down payment by lenders. Up to $60,000 in entitlement may be available to veterans purchasing or constructing homes to be financed with a loan of more than $144,000 and to veterans who obtain an Interest Rate Reduction Refinancing Loan of more than $144,000. The amount of entitlement varies with the loan amount. Loan guaranty limits are listed in the "Tables" section of this booklet.

VA does not establish a maximum loan amount. No loan for the acquisition of a home, however, may exceed the reasonable value of the property, which is based on an appraiser's estimate. A buyer, seller, real estate agent or lender can request a VA appraisal by completing VA Form 26-1805, Request for Determination of Reasonable Value. The requester pays for the appraisal, often called a "VA appraisal," according to a fee schedule approved by VA. This VA appraisal estimates the value of the property, but is not an inspection and does not guarantee that the house is free of defects. VA guarantees the loan, not the condition of the property.

A loan for the purpose of refinancing existing mortgage loans or other liens secured on a dwelling is generally limited to 90 percent of the appraised value of the dwelling. A loan to reduce the interest rate on an existing VA-guaranteed loan, however, can be made for an amount equal to the outstanding balance on the old loan plus closing costs, up to two discount points, and energy- efficient improvements. A loan for the purchase of a manufactured home or lot is limited to 95 percent of the amount that would be subject to finance charges. The VA funding fee and up to $6,000 in energy-efficient improvements also may be included in the loan.

A veteran who previously obtained a VA loan can use the remaining entitlement for a second purchase. The amount of remaining entitlement is the difference between $36,000 ($60,000 for certain loans, as described above) and the amount of entitlement used on prior loans. Remaining entitlement is not necessary for veterans to refinance an existing VA loan with a new one at a lower interest rate.

Required Occupancy

Veterans must certify that they intend to live in the home they are buying or building with a VA guaranty. A veteran who wishes to refinance or improve a home with a VA guaranty also must certify to being in occupancy at the time of application. A spouse may certify occupancy if the buyer is on active duty. In refinancing a VA-guaranteed loan solely to reduce the interest rate, veterans need only certify to prior occupancy.

Closing Costs

Payment in cash is required on all home loan closing costs, including title search and recording, hazard insurance premiums, prepaid taxes and a one percent origination fee, which may be required by lenders in lieu of certain other costs. In the case of refinancing loans, all such costs may be included in the loan, as long as the total loan does not exceed 90 percent of the reasonable value of the property. Interest Rate Reduction Refinancing Loans may include closing costs and a maximum of two discount points. Loans, including refinancing loans, are charged a funding fee by VA, except for loans made to disabled veterans and unremarried surviving spouses of veterans who died as a result of service. The VA funding fee is based on the loan amount and, at the discretion of the veteran and the lender, may be included in the loan. Funding fee rates are listed in the "Tables" section of this booklet.

Financing, Interest Rates and Terms

Veterans obtain VA-guaranteed loans through the usual lending institutions, including banks, savings and loan associations, building and loan associations, and mortgage loan companies. Veterans may obtain a loan with a fixed interest rate, which may be negotiated with the lender. If the lender charges discount points on the loan, the veteran may negotiate with the seller as to who will pay points or if they will be split between buyer and seller. Points paid by the veteran may not be included in the loan, except that a maximum of two points may be included in Interest Rate Reduction Refinancing Loans. The loan may be for as long as 30 years and 32 days.

VA does not require that a down payment be made, except in the following instances: (1) a manufactured home or lot loan; (2) a loan with graduated payment features; and (3) to prevent the amount of a loan from exceeding VA's determination of the property's reasonable value. If the sale price exceeds the reasonable value, the veteran must certify that the difference is being paid in cash without supplementary borrowing. A cash down payment of 5 percent of the purchase price is required for manufactured home or lot loans.

Release of Liability, Loan Assumption

When a veteran sells a home financed through a VA guaranty to a purchaser who assumes the loan, the veteran may request release from liability to the federal government provided the loan is current, the purchaser has been obligated by contract to purchase the property and assume all of the veteran's liabilities, and VA is satisfied that the purchaser is a good risk. A release of liability does not mean that a veteran's guaranty entitlement is restored. If the new veteran-buyer agrees to substitute entitlement for that of the veteran-seller, entitlement may be restored to the veteran-seller.

A VA loan for which a commitment was made on or after March 1, 1988, is not assumable without approval of VA or its authorized agent. The person who assumes a VA loan for which a commitment was made on or after March 1, 1988, must pay a fee to VA equal to one-half of one percent of the balance of the loan being assumed. If a person disposes of the property securing a VA-guaranteed loan for which a commitment was made after March 1, 1988, without first notifying the holder of the loan, the holder may demand immediate and full payment of the loan. Veterans whose loans were closed after Dec. 31, 1989, have no liability to the government following a foreclosure, except in cases involving fraud, misrepresentation or bad faith.

Loans for Native American Veterans

VA direct home loans are available to eligible Native American veterans who wish to purchase, construct or improve a home on Native American trust land. These loans may be used to simultaneously purchase and improve a home. Direct loans also are available to reduce the interest rate on existing loans obtained under this program. VA direct loans may be limited to the cost of the home or $80,000, whichever is less. A funding fee must be paid to VA. The fee is 1.25 percent for loans to purchase, construct or improve a home. For loans to refinance an existing loan, the fee is 0.5 percent of the loan amount. Veterans receiving compensation for service-connected disability are not required to pay the funding fee. The funding fee may be paid in cash or included in the loan. The following may not be included in the loan: VA appraisal, credit report, loan processing fee, title search, title insurance, recording fees, transfer taxes, survey charges or hazard insurance.

Repossessed Homes

VA sells homes that have been acquired after foreclosure of a VA-guaranteed loan. These homes are available to both veterans and nonveterans. Contact local real estate agents for available listings or check the Property Management section of VA's home loan guarantee website for listings and additional information (http://www.homeloans.va.gov/).

Safeguards for Veterans

The following home loan guarantee safeguards have been established to protect veterans:

1. Homes completed less than a year before purchase with VA financing and inspected during construction by either VA or HUD must meet VA requirements.

2. VA may suspend from the loan program those who take unfair advantage of veteran borrowers or decline to sell a new home or make a loan because of race, color, religion, sex, disability, family status or national origin.

3. The builder of a new home is required to give the purchasing veteran a one-year warranty that the home has been constructed to VA-approved plans and specifications. A similar warranty must be given for new manufactured homes.

4. In cases of new construction completed under VA or HUD inspection, VA may pay or otherwise compensate a veteran borrower for correction of structural defects seriously affecting livability if assistance is requested within four years of a home-loan guaranty.

5. The borrower obtaining a loan may only be charged the fees and other charges prescribed by VA as allowable.

6. The borrower can prepay without penalty the entire loan or any part not less than the amount of one installment or $100.

7. VA encourages holders to extend forbearance if a borrower becomes temporarily unable to meet the terms of the loan.

Children with Spina Bifida

Spina bifida patients who are children of Vietnam veterans may be eligible for vocational training, health care, and a monthly allowance.

Vocational Training.
The Vocational Rehabilitation and Employment program administers a vocational training program to enable a qualified child to prepare for and attain suitable employment. Services may include counseling and rehabilitative services, education, training and employment services leading to suitable employment. VA pays for the cost of these services.

Eligibility
To qualify for entitlement to a vocational training program, an applicant must be a child:

1. to whom VA has awarded a monthly allowance for spina bifida, and
2. for whom VA has determined that achievement of a vocational goal is reasonably feasible.

A vocational training program may not begin before a child's 18th birthday or the date the child completes secondary schooling, whichever comes first. Depending on the need, a child may be provided up to 24 months of full-time training.

Spina Bifida Allowance
The monthly allowance is set at three levels, depending upon the degree of disability suffered by the child. The three levels are based on neurological manifestations that define the severity of disability: impairment of the functioning of the extremities, impairment of bowel or bladder function, and impairment of intellectual functioning. Allowances for 2002 can be found in the "Tables" section of this booklet. Contact a VA regional office to apply for medical treatment or benefits payments.

Life Insurance

Two regular and two disabled insurance programs are currently open for new policyholders. Servicemembers' Group Life Insurance is open to active-duty members and reservists of the uniformed services. Veterans' Group Life Insurance is available to individuals released from active duty after Aug. 1, 1974, and to separated reservists. Service-Disabled Veterans Insurance is available for veterans with service-connected disabilities. Veterans' Mortgage Life Insurance provides mortgage life insurance for veterans who are eligible for specially adapted housing grants.

Servicemembers' Group Life Insurance
The following are automatically insured for $250,000 under Service-members' Group Life Insurance (SGLI): active-duty members of the Army, Navy, Air Force, Marines and Coast Guard; commissioned members of the National Oceanic and Atmospheric Administration and the Public Health Service; cadets or midshipmen of the service academies; members, cadets and midshipmen of the ROTC while engaged in authorized training; members of the Ready Reserves; and members who volunteer for assignment to a mobilization category in the Individual Ready Reserve. Individuals may elect to be covered for a lesser amount or not to be covered at all. Part-time coverage may be provided to members of the Reserves who do not qualify for full-time coverage. Premiums are deducted automatically from an individual's pay or are collected by the individual's service branch.

Veterans' Group Life Insurance
SGLI may be converted to Veterans' Group Life Insurance (VGLI), which provides renewable five-year term coverage. The Office of Servicemembers' Group Life Insurance, 290 W. Mt. Pleasant Ave., Livingston, NJ 07039-2747, administers this program. VGLI is available to: (a) individuals with full-time SGLI coverage upon release from active duty or the Reserves; (b) individuals with part-time SGLI coverage who incur a disability or aggravate a pre-existing disability during a reserve period which renders them uninsurable at standard premium rates; and (c) members of the Individual Ready Reserve and Inactive National Guard.

Individuals entitled to SGLI coverage can convert to VGLI by submitting the premium within 120 days of separating from active duty or the reserves. After 121 days, the individual may be granted VGLI provided an initial premium and evidence of insurability are submitted within one year after termination of the individual's SGLI coverage. Individuals with full-time SGLI coverage who are totally disabled at the time of separation and whose service makes them eligible for VGLI may purchase the insurance while remaining totally disabled up to one year following separation.

Accelerated Death Benefits for SGLI and VGLI

A member insured under SGLI or VGLI program, if terminally ill (prognosis of nine months or less to live), may apply for up to 50 percent of the coverage amount in advance.

Service-Disabled Veterans Insurance

A veteran who has a service-connected disability but is otherwise in good health may apply to VA for up to $10,000 in life insurance coverage at standard insurance rates within two years from the date of being notified of service-connected status. This insurance is limited to veterans who left service after April 24, 1951. Veterans who are totally disabled may apply for a waiver of premiums. For those veterans who are eligible for this waiver, additional coverage of up to $20,000 is available. Premiums cannot be waived on the additional insurance.

Veterans' Mortgage Life Insurance

The maximum amount of mortgage life insurance available for those who are eligible for a specially adapted housing grant is $90,000. Protection is automatic unless the veteran declines or does not provide sufficient mortgage information upon which to issue insurance. Premiums are automatically deducted from VA benefit payments or paid direct, if the veteran does not draw compensation, and will continue until the mortgage has been liquidated, the home is sold, or the coverage terminates when the veteran reaches age 70. If a mortgage is disposed of, VMLI may be obtained on the mortgage of another home.

Insurance Dividends

Active government life insurance policies beginning with the letters V, RS, W, J, JR, JS or K, automatically pay dividends annually on the policy anniversary date. Policyholders do not need to apply for these dividends, but may select from a number of options for how they should be handled. VA insurance dividends, and interest on dividends left on deposit or credit with VA, are not taxable. For more information, visit the VA Life Insurance Program Web page (http://www.insurance.va.gov) or contact the VA Insurance Center at 1-800-669-8477.

Persistent rumors about special SGLI or VGLI dividends and dividends for holders of lapsed policies are not true.

Miscellaneous Insurance Information

Increasing Insurance. Policyholders with National Service Life Insurance, Veterans Special Life Insurance and Veterans Reopened Insurance can use their dividends to purchase additional paid-up coverage.

Reinstating Lapsed Insurance. Lapsed term policies may be reinstated within five years from the date of lapse. Contact the VA Insurance Center for details. A five-year term policy that is not lapsed at the end of the term period is automatically renewed for an additional five-year period. Lapsed permanent plan policies may be reinstated within certain time limits and with certain health requirements. Reinstated policies require repayment of all back premiums, plus interest.

Converting Term Policies. A term policy that is in force may be converted to a permanent plan. Upon reaching renewal at age 70 or older, National Service Life Insurance term policies on total disability premium waiver are automatically converted to permanent insurance, which provides cash and loan values and higher dividends.

Cash Value for Term Capped Policies. Since Sept. 11, 2000, policyholders of National Service Life Insurance and Veterans Special Life Insurance whose term policies are capped at renewal age 70, have cash values associated with their policies. Policyholders who voluntarily cancel their policies may either take the cash value or use it to purchase paid-up insurance.

Modified Life Policy. A "modified life at age 65" plan is available to National Service Life Insurance policyholders. The premium rates for this plan remain the same throughout the premium-payment period, while the face value reduces by 50 percent at age 65. The reduced amount may be replaced with a "special ordinary life policy." A "modified life at age 70" plan also is available.

Disability Provisions. National Service Life Insurance policyholders who become totally disabled should consult VA about premium waivers.

Borrowing on Policies. Policyholders may borrow up to 94 percent of the cash surrender value of their insurance and continue the insurance in force by payment of premiums. Interest on policy loans is compounded annually. The current interest rate may be obtained at any VA office, or by calling toll-free 1-800-669-8477.

For additional information about government life insurance, call the VA Insurance Center in Philadelphia toll-free, 1-800-669-8477. Specialists are available between the hours of 8:30 a.m. and 6 p.m., Eastern Time, to discuss premium payments, insurance dividends, address changes, policy loans, naming beneficiaries and reporting the death of the insured. After hours, a caller may leave a recorded message, which will be answered on the next workday, or may use the Interactive Voice Response system.

If the insurance policy number is not known, send whatever information is available, such as the veteran's VA file number, date of birth, social security number, military serial number or military service branch and dates of service to:

> Department of Veterans Affairs
> Regional Office and Insurance Center
> Box 42954
> Philadelphia, PA 19101

Burial Benefits

Burial in National Cemeteries

VA Cemeteries: Service members who die while on active duty and veterans discharged under conditions other than dishonorable are eligible for burial in a VA national cemetery. With certain exceptions, service beginning after September 7, 1980, as an enlisted person, and after October 16, 1981, as an officer, must be for a minimum of 24 consecutive months or the full period for which the person was called to active duty. Reservists and National Guard members are eligible if they were entitled to retired pay at the time of death, or would have been entitled had they not been under the age of 60.

Certain Filipino veterans of World War II, to include Philippine Commonwealth Army veterans and veterans of organized guerilla forces may be eligible if the veteran, at time of death, was a citizen of the United States or an alien lawfully admitted for permanent residence in the United States who had resided in the United States.

Persons convicted of a Federal or State capital crime, and sentenced to death or life imprisonment without parole, are barred by law from being buried or memorialized in a VA national cemetery or in Arlington National Cemetery.

Spouses and minor children of service members and eligible veterans also may be buried in a national cemetery. Minor children are those under 21 years of age, or under 23 years of age if pursuing a course of instruction at an approved educational institution. Unmarried adult children of eligible persons who are physically or mentally disabled and incapable of self-support also are eligible for burial. If a surviving spouse of an eligible veteran marries a nonveteran, and that subsequent marriage was terminated by the nonveteran's death or dissolved by annulment or divorce, the surviving spouse is eligible for burial in a national cemetery.

Gravesites in national cemeteries cannot be reserved. The funeral director or the next of kin makes interment arrangements for an eligible veteran or dependent at the time of need by contacting the national cemetery in which burial is desired. Reservations made under previous programs are honored. VA normally does not conduct burials on weekends. However, weekend callers will be directed to one of three VA cemetery offices that remain open during weekends to schedule burials for the following week at all national cemeteries.

Arlington National Cemetery: Arlington National Cemetery is operated by the Department of the Army. Eligibility for burials is more limited than at other national cemeteries. Information on Arlington National Cemetery burials may be found on the Internet (http://www.mdw.army.mil/fs-a01.htm), by writing to Superintendent, Arlington National Cemetery, Arlington, VA 22211, or calling 703-695-3250.

Department of the Interior and State Veterans Cemeteries: The two active national cemeteries administered by the Department of the Interior are Andersonville National Cemetery in Georgia and Andrew Johnson National Cemetery in Tennessee. Eligibility for burial is similar to VA cemetery eligibility. Cemeteries for veterans also are operated by many states. Contact the state cemetery or state veterans affairs office, as the eligibility requirements for these cemeteries may differ from those for national cemeteries.

Headstones and Markers

Upon request, VA furnishes headstones or markers at no charge for graves in cemeteries around the world for service members who die while on active duty and for eligible veterans. VA also provides headstones or markers for spouses and dependents buried in military, state or national veterans cemeteries, but not for those buried in private cemeteries. Flat bronze, granite or marble markers and upright granite and marble headstones are available. The style chosen must be consistent with existing monuments at the place of burial. Niche markers also are available to mark columbaria used for inurnment of cremated remains.

Government-furnished headstones and markers must be inscribed with the name of the deceased, branch of service, and the year of birth and death, in this order. Headstones and markers also may be inscribed with other items, including an authorized emblem of belief and, space permitting, additional text including military grade, rate or rank, war service such as "World War II", complete dates of birth and death, military awards, military organizations and civilian or veteran affiliations. When burial or memorialization is in a national, state or military veterans cemetery, the headstone or marker must be ordered through cemetery officials. To apply and to obtain specific information on available styles, contact the cemetery where the headstone or marker is to be placed.

When burial occurs in a private cemetery, an application for a government-furnished headstone or marker must be made to VA. The government will ship the headstone or marker free of charge, but will not pay for its placement. To apply, mail a completed VA Form 40-1330, Application for Standard Government Headstone or Marker for Installation in a Private or State Veterans Cemetery, along with a copy of the veteran's military service discharge document to Memorial Programs Service (403), Department of Veterans Affairs, 810 Vermont Avenue, NW, Washington, DC, 20420-0001. Do not send original discharge documents, as they will not be returned.

Memorial Headstones or Markers

VA provides memorial headstones and markers, bearing the inscription "In Memory of" as their first line, to memorialize eligible veterans and dependents whose remains were not recovered or identified, were buried at sea, donated to science or cremated and scattered. To be memorialized, dependents do not need to outlive the veteran from whom their eligibility is based.

Memorial headstones or markers must be placed in national, state veterans, local or private cemeteries. VA supplies and ships memorial headstones and markers free of cost for placement in state, local and private cemeteries, but does not pay for their plots or placement.

Presidential Memorial Certificates

Certificates signed by the president are issued upon request to recognize the military service of honorably discharged deceased veterans. Next of kin, other relatives and friends may request Presidential Memorial Certificates in person at any VA regional office or by mail: Department of Veterans Affairs, National Cemetery Administration (403A), 810 Vermont Avenue, NW, Washington, DC 20420-0001. There is no pre-printed form to complete or time limit for requesting these certificates, but requests should include a copy, not the original, of the deceased veteran's discharge document and clearly indicate to what address the certificate should be sent. Additional information and a sample certificate can be found on the Internet (http://www.cem.va.gov/pmc.htm) .

Military Funeral Honors

Upon request, the Department of Defense will provide military funeral honors for the burial of military members and eligible veterans. A basic military funeral honors ceremony consists of the folding and presentation of the United States flag and the playing of Taps by a bugler, if available, or by electronic recording. A funeral honors detail to perform this ceremony consists of two or more uniformed members of the armed forces, with at least one member from the service in which the deceased veteran served.

Military members on active duty or in the Selected Reserve are eligible for military funeral honors. Also eligible are former military members who served on active duty and departed under conditions other than dishonorable, former members of the Selected Reserve who completed at least one term of enlistment or period of initial obligated service and departed under conditions other than dishonorable, and former military members discharged from the Selected Reserve due to a disability incurred or aggravated in the line of duty.

The Department of Defense maintains a toll-free telephone line (1-877-MIL-HONR) for use by funeral directors only to request honors. Family members should inform their funeral directors if they desire military funeral honors for a veteran. VA national cemetery staff can help arrange for honors during burials at VA national cemeteries. Veterans service organizations or volunteer groups may help provide honors. For more information, visit the military funeral honors Web page (http://www.militaryfuneralhonors.osd.mil).

Burial Flags
VA provides a United States flag to drape the casket or accompany the urn of a deceased veteran who:
    1. served in any war;
    2. died while on active duty;
    3. served after Jan. 31, 1955;
    4. served at least one enlistment or had been discharged or released from active service for a disability incurred or aggravated in the line of duty;
    5. was entitled to retired pay for service in the National Guard or Reserves at the time of death, or would have been entitled to retired pay, but for being under 60 years of age.

Veterans separated from the service must have been discharged or released under conditions other than dishonorable. After the funeral service, the flag may be given to the next of kin, close friend or associate of the deceased veteran. Burial flags may be obtained at VA regional offices, national cemeteries and most local post offices. Only one flag is authorized for each veteran.

Reimbursement of Burial Expenses

VA will pay a burial allowance up to $2,000 if the veteran's death is service-connected. In some instances, VA also will pay the cost of transporting the remains of a service-disabled veteran to the national cemetery nearest the home of the deceased that has available gravesites. In such cases, the person who bore the veteran's burial expenses may claim reimbursement from VA. There is no time limit for filing reimbursement claims in service-connected death cases.

VA will pay a $300 burial and funeral expense allowance for veterans who, at time of death, were entitled to receive pension or compensation or would have been entitled to compensation but for receipt of military retirement pay. Eligibility also may be established when death occurs in a VA facility, a nursing home under VA contract or a state veterans nursing home. Additional costs of transportation of the remains may be paid. In nonservice-connected death cases, claims must be filed within two years after permanent burial or cremation.

VA will pay a $300 plot allowance when a veteran is not buried in a cemetery that is under U.S. government jurisdiction under the following circumstances: the veteran was discharged from active duty because of disability incurred or aggravated in the line of duty; the veteran was in receipt of compensation or pension or would have been except for receiving military retired pay; or the veteran died in a VA facility. The $300 plot allowance may be paid to the state if a veteran is buried without charge for the cost of a plot or interment in a state-owned cemetery reserved solely for veteran burials. Burial expenses paid by the deceased's employer or a state agency will not be reimbursed. For information on monetary benefits, call 1-800-827-1000.

Additional information about burial and memorial benefits may be obtained at any VA national cemetery, regional office or on the Internet (http://www.cem.va.gov/). To check on the status of an application for headstone or marker, call 1-800-697-6947.

Survivor Benefits

Dependency and Indemnity Compensation (DIC)

Dependency and Indemnity Compensation (DIC) payments may be available for surviving spouses who have not remarried, unmarried children under 18, helpless children, those between 18 and 23 if attending a VA-approved school, and low-income parents of deceased service members or veterans. To be eligible, the deceased must have died from: (1) a disease or injury incurred or aggravated while on active duty or active duty for training; (2) an injury incurred or aggravated in line of duty while on inactive duty training; or (3) a disability compensable by VA. Death cannot be the result of willful misconduct. If a spouse remarries, eligibility for benefits may be restored if the marriage is terminated later by death, annulment or divorce.

DIC payments also may be authorized for survivors of veterans who were totally service-connected disabled when they died, even though their service-connected disabilities did not cause their deaths. The survivor qualifies if: (1) the veteran was continuously rated totally disabled for a period of 10 or more years immediately preceding death; (2) the veteran was so rated for a period of at least five years from the date of military discharge; or (3) the veteran was a former prisoner of war who died after Sept. 30, 1999, and who was continuously rated totally disabled for a period of at least one year immediately preceding death. Payments under this provision are subject to offset by the amount received from judicial proceedings brought on account of the veteran's death. The discharge must have been under conditions other than dishonorable.

DIC Payments to Surviving Spouse

Surviving spouses of veterans who died after Jan. 1, 1993, receive $935 a month. For a spouse entitled to DIC based on the veteran's death prior to Jan. 1, 1993, the amount paid is $935 or an amount based on the veteran's pay grade. See the "Tables" section of this booklet for more information.

DIC Payments to Parents and Children

The monthly payment for parents of deceased veterans depends upon their income. There are additional DIC payments for dependent children. A child may be eligible if there is no surviving spouse, and the child is unmarried and under age 18, or if the child is between the ages of 18 and 23 and attending school. See the "Tables" section of this booklet for more information on DIC for children.

Special Allowances
Surviving spouses and parents receiving DIC may be granted a special allowance to pay for aid and attendance by another person if they are patients in a nursing home or require the regular assistance of another person. Surviving spouses receiving DIC may be granted a housebound special allowance if they are permanently house-bound. The current allowances for spouses are shown in the "Tables" section of this booklet.

Restored Entitlement Program for Survivors
Survivors of veterans who died of service-connected causes incurred or aggravated prior to Aug. 13, 1981, may be eligible for special benefits. This benefit is similar to the benefits for students and surviving spouses with children between ages 16 and 18 that were eliminated from Social Security benefits. The benefits are payable in addition to any other benefits to which the family may be entitled. The amount of the benefit is based on information provided by the Social Security Administration.

Death Pension
Pensions based on need are available for surviving spouses and unmarried children of deceased veterans with wartime service. Spouses must not have remarried and children must be under age 18, or under age 23 if attending a VA-approved school. Pension is not payable to those with estates large enough to provide mainte-nance. The veteran must have been discharged under conditions other than dishonorable and must have had 90 days or more of active military service, at least one day of which was during a period of war, or a service-connected disability justifying discharge for disability. If the veteran died in service but not in line of duty, benefits may be payable if the veteran had completed at least two years of honorable service. Children who became incapable of self-support because of a disability before age 18 may be eligible for a pension as long as the condition exists, unless the child marries or the child's income exceeds the applicable limit. A surviving spouse may be entitled to higher income limitations or additional benefits if living in a nursing home, in need of aid and attendance by another person or permanently housebound.

The Improved Pension program provides a monthly payment to bring an eligible person's income to a support level established by law. The payment is reduced by the annual income from other sources such as Social Security paid to the surviving spouse or dependent children. Medical expenses may be deducted from the income ceiling. Pension is not payable to those who have assets that can be used to provide adequate maintenance. Maximum rates for the Improved Death Pension are shown in the "Tables" section of this booklet.

Dependents' Education

Educational assistance benefits are available to spouses who have not remarried and children of: (1) veterans who died or are permanently and totally disabled as the result of a disability arising from active military service; (2) veterans who died from any cause while rated permanently and totally disabled from service-connected disability; (3) service members listed for more than 90 days as currently missing in action or captured in line of duty by a hostile force; (4) service members listed for more than 90 days as currently detained or interned by a foreign government or power.

The termination of a surviving spouse's remarriage — by death, divorce, or ceasing to live with another person as that person's spouse — will reinstate Dependents' Educational Assistance benefits to the surviving spouse.

Benefits may be awarded for pursuit of associate, bachelor or graduate degrees at colleges and universities — including independent study, cooperative training and study abroad programs. Courses leading to a certificate or diploma from business, technical or vocational schools also may be taken.

Benefits may be awarded for apprenticeships, on-the-job training programs and farm cooperative courses. Benefits for correspondence courses under certain conditions are available to spouses only. Secondary-school programs may be pursued if the individual is not a high-school graduate. An individual with a deficiency in a subject may receive tutorial assistance benefits if enrolled halftime or more. Deficiency, refresher and other training also may be available.

Monthly Payments: Payments are made monthly. The rate is $670 a month for full-time school attendance, with lesser amounts for part-time training. A person may receive educational assistance for full-time training for up to 45 months or the equivalent in part-time training. Payments to a spouse end 10 years from the date the individual is found eligible or from the date of the death of the veteran. VA may grant an extension. Children generally must be between the ages of 18 and 26 to receive education benefits, though extensions may be granted.

Work-Study: Participants must train at the three-quarter or full-time rate. They may be paid in advance 40 percent of the amount specified in the work-study agreement or an amount equal to 50 times the applicable minimum wage, whichever is less. Participants under the supervision of a VA employee may provide outreach services, prepare and process VA paperwork, and work at a VA medical facility or perform other approved activities. They may also help at national or state veterans' cemeteries in addition to assisting in outreach services furnished by State Approving Agencies

Counseling Services: VA may provide counseling services to help an eligible dependent pursue an educational or vocational objective.

Special Benefits: An eligible child over age 14 with a physical or mental disability that impairs pursuit of an educational program may receive special restorative training to lessen or overcome that impairment. This training may include speech and voice correction, language retraining, lip reading, auditory training, Braille reading and writing, and similar programs. Certain disabled or surviving spouses are also eligible for special restorative training. Specialized vocational training also is available to an eligible spouse or child over age 14 who is handicapped by a physical or mental disability that prevents pursuit of an educational program.

Spina Bifida Assistance: A child with spina bifida, parented by a Vietnam veteran, can receive vocational training to guide the child, parent or guardian in choosing a vocational training program. VA also will provide up to 24 months of training to achieve a vocational goal.

Educational Loans
Loans are available to spouses who qualify for educational assistance. Spouses who have passed their 10-year period of eligibility may be eligible for an educational loan. During the first two years after the end of their eligibility period, they may borrow up to $2,500 per academic year to continue a full-time course leading to a college degree or to a professional or vocational objective that requires at least six months to complete. VA may waive the six-month requirement. Loans are based on financial need.

Home Loan Guaranties

A VA loan guaranty to acquire a home may be available to an unmarried spouse of a veteran or service member who died as a result of service-connected disabilities, or to a spouse of a service member who has been officially listed as missing in action or as a prisoner of war for more than 90 days. Spouses of those listed as prisoners of war or missing in action are limited to one loan.

Montgomery GI Bill Death Benefit

VA will pay a special Montgomery GI Bill death benefit to a designated survivor in the event of the service-connected death of an individual while on active duty or within one year after discharge or release. The deceased must either have been entitled to educational assistance under the Montgomery GI Bill program or a participant in the program who would have been so entitled but for the high school diploma or length-of-service requirement. The amount paid will be equal to the participant's actual military pay reduction (discussed on page 22 of this booklet), less any education benefits paid.

Women Veterans

Women veterans are eligible for the same VA benefits as male veterans. However, additional gender-specific services and benefits are available for women veterans, including breast and pelvic examinations and other general reproductive health-care services. VA provides preventive health care counseling, contraceptive services, menopause management, Pap smears and mammography. Referrals are made for services that VA is unable to provide. Women Veterans' Coordinators are available in a private setting at all VA facilities to assist women veterans seeking treatment and benefits.

VA health-care professionals provide counseling and treatment to help veterans overcome psychological trauma resulting from sexual trauma during active military service. Appropriate care and services are provided for any injury, illness or psychological condition resulting from such trauma.

Homeless Veterans

A number of VA benefits, including disability compensation, pension and education benefits, can prevent at-risk veterans from becoming homeless. VA conducts community-based "stand downs" to make benefits information and assistance more accessible to homeless veterans. Homeless veterans also are provided special assistance through other VA program initiatives.

VA provides health and rehabilitation programs for homeless veterans. Health Care for Homeless Veterans programs provide outreach and comprehensive medical, psychological and rehabilitation treatment programs. Domiciliary Care for Homeless Veterans programs provide residential rehabilitation services. VA supports Compensated Work Therapy/Therapeutic Residence group homes, special daytime, drop-in centers, and Comprehensive Homeless Centers.

VA's Homeless Providers Grant and Per Diem Program assists nonprofit and local government agencies to establish housing or service centers for homeless veterans. Grants are awarded for the construction, acquisition or renovation of facilities. VA also works with the Department of Housing and Urban Development, the Social Security Administration, veterans service organizations, and community nonprofit groups to assist homeless veterans. For information on benefits for homeless veterans, contact the nearest VA facility.

More information about this program, including information about VA loan guarantees for construction or rehabilitation of multifamily transitional housing for homeless veterans, can be found on the Internet (http://www.va.gov/health/homeless/).

Overseas Benefits

Medical Benefits

VA will pay for medical services for the treatment of service-connected disabilities and related conditions for veterans living or traveling outside the U.S. Before using the program, veterans living in Canada should register with the VA Center in White River Junction, VT 05009-0001, USA, phone 802-296-6379. Those living in the Philippines should register with the U.S. VA office in Pasay City, phone 011-632-833-4566. All other veterans living outside the U.S. should register with the Denver Foreign Medical Program office, P.O. Box 65021, Denver, CO 80206-9021, USA, phone 303-331-7590. Outside the United States, VA pays for nursing-home care only in the Philippines.

Other Overseas Benefits

VA monetary benefits, including compensation, pension, educational assistance and burial allowances, generally are payable overseas. Some programs in foreign jurisdictions are restricted. Home-loan guaranties are available only in the United States and selected U.S. territories and possessions. Educational benefits are limited to approved degree-granting programs in institutions of higher learning. Beneficiaries residing in foreign countries should contact the nearest American embassy or consulate for information and claims assistance. In Canada, veterans should contact an office of Veterans Affairs Canada. Additional information on benefits and services available outside the United States can be found on the World Wide Web (http://www.vba.va.gov/foreign/).

Small and Disadvantaged Businesses

VA's Office of Small and Disadvantaged Business Utilization (OSDBU) helps small businesses obtain information on acquisition opportunities with VA. Like other Federal offices, VA is required to place a portion of its contracts and purchases with small and disadvantaged businesses. For more information, write to OSDBU, U.S. Department of Veterans Affairs (OOSB), 810 Vermont Avenue, N.W., Washington, D.C. 20420-0001, call 1-800-949-8387 toll-free, or visit the OSDBU Web site at: http://www.va.gov/osdbu.

OSDBU's Center for Veterans Enterprise (CVE) helps veterans interested in forming or expanding small businesses. The CVE helps VA contracting offices identify veteran-owned small businesses and works with the Small Business Administration's Veterans Business Development Officers and Small Business Development Centers nationwide regarding veterans' business financing, management and technical assistance needs. For more information, write to CVE, U.S. Department of Veterans Affairs (OOVE), 810 Vermont Avenue, N.W., Washington, D.C. 20420-0001, call 1-800-949-8387 toll-free, or visit the CVE web site (http://www.vetbiz.gov).

Workplace Benefits

Some benefits for veterans and their dependents are administered by agencies other than the Department of Veterans Affairs. The following information describes these benefits and how to apply for them.

Unemployment Compensation

Weekly unemployment compensation may be paid to discharged service members for a limited period of time. The amount and duration of payments are determined by individual states. To apply, veterans who do not begin civilian employment immediately after leaving military service should contact their nearest state employment office and present a copy of their military discharge, form DD-214.

Transition Assistance Program

The Transition Assistance Program (TAP) assists service members and their spouses who are scheduled for separation from active duty. The program, a joint effort by the Departments of Defense, Labor (DoL), Transportation and Veterans Affairs, provides employment and training information to service members within 180 days of their separation from the military. Together with the military services, these agencies offer a number of services and benefits designed to equip separating service members with the basic job-hunting skills, tools and self-confidence necessary to successfully find employment in the civilian workforce. The programs described below were developed through the combined efforts of these agencies.

TAP Workshops

Three-day workshops to help separating service members and their spouses make the transition from military to civilian employment are conducted at military installations. Disabled service members also are provided employment counseling during this workshop. More information can be found on the DoL Veterans' Employment and Training Service Web page (www2.dol.gov/dol/vets), by contacting the Veterans' Employment Service Representative at the nearest state employment service office (listed in the phone book under U.S. Government, Labor Department) or the Transition Office at the nearest military base.

Pre-separation Counseling

The military services are required by law to provide individual pre-separation counseling at least 90 days prior to each service member's discharge. These sessions present information on education, training, employment assistance, Guard and Reserve programs, medical benefits and financial assistance to separating service members.

Verification of Military Experience and Training

The Verification of Military Experience and Training (VMET) Document, DD Form 2586, is provided to all eligible departing service members. The document helps service members verify previous experience and training to potential employers, write their resumes, prepare for job interviews, negotiate credits at schools, and obtain certificates or licenses. The military departments make the VMET document available by mail and on the Internet (http://www.dmdc.osd.mil/vmet), from which service members can view it online or print locally. Service members should receive their DD Form 2586 between 90 and 180 days prior to separation.

Transition Bulletin Board (TBB)

This web site (http://www.dmdc.osd.mil/ot) allows employers to make advertisements for short-term or long-term jobs available online. In addition, the TBB contains business opportunities, a calendar of transition seminars, job fairs, information on military and veterans associations, transition products and services, training and educational opportunities, as well as other announcements pertinent to separating personnel.

DoD Transportal

This DoD Web site (http://www.dodtransportal.org) supplements the various TAP program resources available to separating military personnel. In addition to providing the locations and phone numbers of all Transition Assistance Offices, the site offers mini-courses on conducting successful job search campaigns, writing resumes, using the Internet to find a job and links to job search and recruiting Web sites. A DoD job search Web site (http://www.dod.jobsearch.org) features online resume entry, job advertisements and referrals.

Veterans' Workforce Investment Program

The Veterans' Workforce Investment Program provides employment and training programs to increase employment, job retention, earnings, and occupational skills of recently separated veterans and veterans who have service-connected disabilities, significant barriers to employment or who served on active duty in the armed forces during a campaign or expedition for which a campaign badge has been authorized.

These programs may be conducted through state or local public agencies, community-based organizations or private, nonprofit organizations. Job counseling, resume preparation, job development and placement services are also available to help homeless veterans re-enter the workforce. Veterans should contact their nearest state employment service office for more information.

State Employment Services

In addition to providing unemployment compensation information, Workforce Career or One-Stop Centers provide a variety of services for veterans seeking employment, including current employment information, education and training opportunities, job counseling and job search workshops and resume preparation assistance. Disabled Veterans Outreach Program specialists at these offices and at VA regional offices and readjustment counseling centers (Vet Centers) work closely with employers, veterans service organizations, community-based organizations and other government agencies to promote job development and improve employment and training opportunities for disabled veterans.

Re-employment Rights

A person who left a civilian job to enter active duty in the Armed Forces may be entitled to return to the job after discharge or release from active duty. Re-employment rights are provided for those who served in the active duty or reserve components of the Armed Forces. To be re-employed, four requirements must be met: (1) the person must give advance notice of military service to the employer; (2) the cumulative absence from the civilian job shall not exceed five years (with some exceptions); (3) the person must submit a timely application for re-employment; and (4) the person must not have been released with a dishonorable or other punitive discharge.

The law calls for the returning veteran to be placed in the job as if the veteran had remained continuously employed. This means that the person may be entitled to benefits that are based on seniority, such as pensions, pay increases and promotions. The law also prohibits discrimination in hiring, promotion or other advantages of employment on the basis of military service.

Applications for re-employment should be given, verbally or in writing, to a person authorized to represent the company for hiring purposes. A record should be kept of the application. If there are problems gaining re-employment, the employee should contact the Department of Labor's Veterans' Employment and Training Service (VETS) in the state of the employer concerned. This applies to private sector, as well as state, local and federal government employees, including the Postal Service.

Employees should contact their agency personnel office if they have questions about their employment restoration rights. If a veteran is not re-employed or is not re-employed properly, the veteran has the right to file a complaint with VETS. Additionally, federal employees may appeal directly to the Merit Systems Protection Board. Non-federal employees may file complaints in U.S. district court. Additional information is available on the Internet (http://www.dol.gov/dol/vets) from the Department of Labor.

Federal Contractor Affirmative Action

Federal legislation prohibits employers with a federal contract of $25,000 or more from discriminating in employment against veterans who separated from active duty within the previous twelve months and those who served on active duty during a war or in a campaign or expedition for which a campaign badge has been authorized. This prohibition also applies to Vietnam Era veterans who served on active duty for more than 180 days, any part of which occurred during the period listed in the "Introduction" section of this booklet, who were discharged or released with other than a dishonorable discharge or with a service-connected disability.

Federal legislation also prohibits employers with federal contracts from discriminating in employment against "special disabled" veterans. Special disabled veterans are veterans who have a VA disability rating of 30 percent or more, veterans who are rated at 10 or 20 percent who have been determined to have a serious employment handicap and veterans who were discharged or released from active duty because of a service-connected disability. Federal legislation requires these contractors to take affirmative action to employ and advance in employment campaign veterans, Vietnam Era and special disabled veterans. It also requires these contractors to list jobs, including full-time, temporary and part-time jobs, with state employment services. Veterans who believe their rights have been violated may file a complaint with the U.S. Department of Labor's

Veterans' Employment and Training Service or at a state employment office.

Federal Jobs for Veterans

The Veterans Readjustment Appointment (VRA) authority allows federal agencies to appoint eligible veterans to jobs without competition. Such appointments may lead to conversion to career or career-conditional employment upon satisfactory work for two years. Veterans seeking VRA appointment should apply directly to the agency where they wish to work.

The Office of Personnel Management (OPM) administers the Disabled Veterans Affirmative Action Program, which requires that all federal departments and agencies establish plans to facilitate the recruitment and advancement of disabled veterans.

Certain veterans, principally those who are disabled or who served in a hostile area, are entitled to preference in competing for civil service jobs. This preference includes five or 10 points added to passing scores in examinations and preference in job retention. Preference also is provided for certain unremarried widows and widowers of deceased veterans and for mothers of military personnel who died in service; spouses of service-connected disabled veterans who are no longer able to work in their usual occupations; and mothers of veterans who have permanent and total service-connected disabilities. Individuals interested in federal employment should contact the personnel offices of the federal agencies in which they wish to be employed. Information also may be obtained by contacting any OPM Service Center. The centers are listed in telephone books under U.S. Government.

Individuals eligible for veterans' preference and honorably discharged veterans who substantially completed three or more years of continuous active service may compete for certain federal jobs. Federal agencies must allow eligible veterans to apply for jobs when they are accepting applications from individuals outside their own workforces.

OPM provides information on veterans' federal service employment rights and privileges on the Internet (http://www.opm.gov/veterans/). Federal job openings can be found by phone through USA Jobs at 912-757-3000 and on the Internet (http://www.usajobs.opm.gov).

Miscellaneous Programs and Benefits

Loans for Farms and Homes

Loans and guaranties may be provided by the U.S. Department of Agriculture to buy, improve or operate farms. Loans and guaranties are available for housing in towns generally up to 20,000 in population. Applications from veterans have preference. For further information contact Farm Service Agency or Rural Economic and Community Development, U.S. Department of Agriculture, Washington, DC 20250, or apply at local Department of Agriculture offices, usually located in county seats.

FHA Home Mortgage Insurance

The Federal Housing Administration is responsible for the Home Mortgage Insurance Program for Veterans. These home loans can require less of a down payment than other FHA programs. Veterans on active duty are eligible if they enlisted before Sept. 8, 1980, or entered on active duty before Oct. 14, 1982, and were discharged under other than dishonorable conditions with at least 90 days service. Veterans with enlisted service after Sept. 7, 1980, or who entered on active duty after Oct. 16, 1981, must have served at least 24 months unless discharged for hardship or disability. Active duty for training is qualifying service. Submit VA Form 26-8261a to VA to obtain a Certificate of Veteran Status. The lender will submit the certificate to FHA.

Naturalization Preference

Aliens with honorable service in the U.S. Armed Forces during hostilities may be naturalized without having to comply with the general requirements for naturalization. Such aliens must have been lawfully admitted to the United States for permanent residence or have been inducted, enlisted, re-enlisted or extended an enlistment in the armed forces while within the United States, Puerto Rico, Guam, the Virgin Islands of the United States, the Canal Zone, American Samoa, Northern Marianas or Swain's Island. Hostilities must be periods declared by the President. Aliens with honorable service in the U.S. Armed Forces for three years or more during periods not considered a conflict or hostility by Executive Order may be naturalized provided they have been lawfully admitted to the United States for permanent residence. Applications must be made while on active duty or within six months of discharge.

Aliens who have served honorably after Oct. 15, 1978, for at least 12 years may be granted special immigrant status. Aliens who died as a result of wounds incurred or disease contracted during periods of hostilities declared by the President may receive recognition as U.S. citizens. The person's next of kin or other authorized representative may submit an application. This posthumous citizenship is honorary only and does not confer any other benefits to the person's surviving relatives. For assistance, contact the nearest office of the Immigration and Naturalization Service, Justice Department.

Small Business Administration

The Small Business Administration (SBA) provides a number of services that assist veterans who own or are considering starting small businesses. Among the services provided are business training, counseling, mentoring and various loan guarantees. A number of different kinds of loan guarantees are provided to banks and other lending institutions, including Military Reservist Economic Injury Disaster Loans for members of the Reserves and National Guard called to active duty during a period of military conflict. The Office of Veterans Business Development operates various outreach programs and maintains liaison with the Congressionally-established National Veterans Business Development Corporation. SBA monitors and reports on veteran-owned small business participation in federal procurement and seeks to achieve a 3% annual federal contracting procurement goal for service disabled veteran-owned small businesses. Information about SBA's full range of programs and services can be found on the Internet (http://www.sba.gov/VETS/) or by contacting the Veterans Business Development Officer at SBA District Offices. Call 1-800-U-ASK-SBA (1-800-827-5722) to locate the nearest SBA Office, or for more information.

Social Security

Monthly retirement, disability and survivor benefits under Social Security are payable to a veteran and dependents if the veteran has earned enough work credits under the program. Upon the veteran's death, a one-time payment of $255 also may be made to the veteran's spouse or child. In addition, a veteran may qualify at age 65 for Medicare's hospital insurance and medical insurance. Medicare protection also is available to people who have received Social Security disability benefits for 24 months, and to insured people and their dependents who need dialysis or kidney transplants.

Active duty or active duty for training in the U.S. uniformed services has counted toward Social Security since January 1957. Since Jan. 1, 1988, inactive duty for training as a member of Reserve components of the armed forces also counts toward Social Security. Service members and veterans receive an extra $300 credit for each quarter in which they received any basic pay for active duty or active duty for training after 1956 and before 1978. After 1977, a credit of $100 is granted for each $300 of reported wages up to a maximum credit of $1,200. No additional Social Security taxes are withheld from pay for these extra credits. Also, noncontributory Social Security credits of $160 a month may be granted to veterans who served after Sept. 15, 1940, and before 1957, including attendance at service academies. More information is available on the Internet (http://www.ssa.gov/) or by calling l-800-772-1213.

Supplemental Security Income

For those age 65 or older and those who are blind or otherwise disabled, Supplemental Security Income (SSI) may be provided if they have little or no income or resources. States may supplement the federal payments to eligible persons and may disregard additional income. Although VA compensation and pension benefits are counted in determining income for SSI purposes, some income is not counted. Also, not all resources count in determining eligibility. For example, a person's home and the land it is on do not count. Personal effects, household goods, automobiles and life insurance may not count, depending upon their value. Information and assistance in applying for these payments may be obtained at any Social Security office or by calling l-800-772-1213.

Passports to Visit Overseas Cemeteries

"No-fee" passports are available for family members visiting graves or memorialization sites at World War I and World War II cemeteries overseas. Those eligible for such passports include surviving spouses, parents, children, sisters, brothers and guardians of the deceased who are buried or commemorated in American military cemeteries on foreign soil. For additional information, write to the American Battle Monuments Commission, Courthouse Plaza II, Suite 500, 2300 Clarendon Blvd., Arlington, VA 22201, or phone 703-696-6897.

Medals

Medals awarded while in active service are issued by the individual military services if requested by veterans or by the next of kin of deceased veterans. Requests for the issuance or replacement of military service medals, decorations, and awards should be directed to the specific branch of the military in which the veteran served. However, for Air Force (including Army Air Corps) and Army veterans, the National Personnel Records Center verifies the awards to which a veteran is entitled and forwards requests and verification to the appropriate service department for issuance of the medals.

Requests for replacement medals should be submitted on Standard Form 180, "Request Pertaining To Military Records," which may be obtained at VA offices, from veterans organizations or downloaded from the Internet (http://www.vba.va.gov/pubs/otherforms.htm). Standard Form 180 and additional information also can be found on the National Personnel Records Center's Internet pages (http://www.nara.gov/regional/mpr.html).

When requesting medals, type or clearly print the veteran's full name, include the veteran's branch of service, service number or Social Security Number and provide the veteran's exact or approximate dates of military service. The request must contain the signature of the veteran or the signature of the next of kin if the veteran is deceased. If available, include a copy of the discharge or separation document, WDAGO Form 53-55 or DD Form 214.

Review of Discharges

Each of the military services maintains a discharge review board with authority to change, correct, or modify discharges or dismissals that are not issued by a sentence of a general court martial. The board has no authority to address medical discharges. The veteran or, if the veteran is deceased or incompetent, the surviving spouse, next of kin or legal representative may apply for a review of discharge by writing to the military department concerned, using Department of Defense Form 293. This form may be obtained at a VA regional office. However, if the discharge was more than 15 years ago, a veteran must petition the appropriate service Board for Correction of Military Records using Department of Defense Form 149, which is discussed in the "Correction of Military Records" section of this booklet. A discharge review is conducted by a review of an applicant's record and, if requested, by a hearing before the board.

Discharges awarded as a result of unauthorized absence in excess of 180 days make persons ineligible for VA benefits regardless of action taken by discharge review boards, unless VA determines there were compelling circumstances for the absence. Boards for the correction of military records also may consider such cases.

Veterans with disabilities incurred or aggravated during active military service may qualify for medical or related benefits regardless of separation and characterization of service. Veterans separated administratively under other than honorable conditions may request that their discharge be reviewed for possible recharacterization, provided they file their appeal within 15 years of the date of separation. Questions regarding the review of a discharge should be addressed to the appropriate discharge review board at the address listed on Department of Defense Form 293.

Replacing Military Records

If discharge or separation papers are lost, duplicate copies may be obtained by contacting the National Personnel Records Center, Military Personnel Records, 9700 Page Blvd., St. Louis, MO 63132-5100. Specify that a duplicate separation document or discharge is needed. The veteran's full name should be printed or typed so that it can be read clearly, but the request must also contain the signature of the veteran or the signature of the next of kin, if the veteran is deceased. Include branch of service, service number or Social Security number and exact or approximate dates and years of service. Use Standard Form 180, "Request Pertaining To Military Records." (See the "World Wide Web Links" section of this booklet for more information on obtaining this and other federal forms through the Internet, or contact your local VA regional office.) It is not necessary to request a duplicate copy of a veteran's discharge or separation papers solely for the purpose of filing a claim for VA benefits. If complete information about the veteran's service is furnished on the application, VA will obtain verification of service from the National Personnel Records Center or the service department concerned. In a medical emergency, information from a veteran's records may be obtained by phoning the appropriate service: Army, 314-538-4261; Air Force, 314-538-4243; Navy, Marine Corps or Coast Guard, 314-538-4141.

Correction of Military Records

The secretary of a military department, acting through a board for correction of military records, has authority to change any military record when necessary to correct an error or remove an injustice. A correction board may consider applications for correction of a military record, including a review of a discharge issued by courts martial.

62

The veteran, survivor or legal representative generally must file a request for correction within three years after discovery of an alleged error or injustice. The board may excuse failure to file within the prescribed time, however, if it finds it would be in the interest of justice to do so. It is an applicant's responsibility to show why the filing of the application was delayed and why it would be in the interest of justice for the board to consider it despite the delay.

To justify any correction, it is necessary to show to the satisfaction of the board that the alleged entry or omission in the records was in error or unjust. Applications should include all available evidence, such as signed statements of witnesses or a brief of arguments supporting the requested correction. Application is made with DD Form 149, available at VA offices, from veterans organizations or from the Internet (http://web1.whs.osd.mil/icdhome/ddeforms.htm).

Armed Forces Retirement Homes

The following veterans may be eligible to live in one of the two retirement homes operated by the Armed Forces Retirement Home: veterans 60 years of age or older who have completed 20 years or more of active service; veterans incapable of earning a livelihood because of a service-connected disability incurred in the line of duty in the Armed Forces; other veterans incapable of earning a livelihood because of injuries, disease, or disability who served in a war theater during a time of war declared by Congress or who were eligible for hostile fire special pay; veterans who served in the women's component of the armed forces before the enactment of the Women's Armed Services Integration Act of 1948. Veterans are not eligible if they have been convicted of a felony or are not free from alcohol, drug or psychiatric problems.

New residents must be capable of living independently in a dormitory. The Armed Forces Retirement Home is an independent federal agency. For information, write to the Public Affairs Office, U.S. Soldiers' and Airmen's Home, 3700 N. Capitol St. NW, Washington, DC 20317, or phone 1-800-422-9988; or write to U.S. Naval Home, 1800 Beach Drive, Gulfport, MS 39507, or phone 1-800-332-3527.

Commissary and Exchange Privileges

Unlimited exchange and commissary store privileges in the United States are available to honorably discharged veterans with a service-connected disability rated at 100 percent, unremarried surviving spouses of members or retired members of the armed forces, recipients of the Medal of Honor, and their dependents and orphans. Certification of total disability is done by VA. Reservists and their dependents also may be eligible. Privileges overseas are governed by international law and are available only if agreed upon by the foreign government concerned. VA provides assistance in completing DD Form 1172, "Application for Uniformed Services Identification and Privilege Card."

Death Gratuity
Military services provide a death gratuity of $6,000 to a deceased service member's next of kin. The death gratuity is paid for death in active service or for retirees who died within 120 days of retirement as a result of service-connected injury or illness. Parents, brothers or sisters may be provided the gratuity, if designated as next of kin by the deceased. The gratuity is paid by the last military command of the deceased. If the beneficiary is not paid automatically, application may be made to the military service concerned.

Appeals

Veterans and other claimants for VA benefits have the right to appeal decisions made by a VA regional office or medical center. Typical issues appealed are disability compensation, pension, education benefits, recovery of overpayments, medication copayment debts and reimbursement for medical services that were not authorized.

A claimant has one year from the date of the notification of a VA decision to file an appeal. The first step in the appeal process is for a claimant to file a written notice of disagreement with the VA regional office or medical center that made the decision. This is a written statement that a claimant disagrees with VA's decision. Following receipt of the written notice, VA will furnish the claimant a "Statement of the Case" describing what facts, laws and regulations were used in deciding the case. To complete the request for appeal, the claimant must file a "Substantive Appeal" within 60 days of the mailing of the Statement of the Case, or within one year from the date VA mailed its decision, whichever period ends later.

Board of Veterans' Appeals
The Board of Veterans' Appeals, located in Washington, D.C., makes decisions on appeals on behalf of the Secretary of Veterans Affairs.

Although it is not required, a veterans service organization, an agent or an attorney may represent a claimant. Appellants may present their case in person to a member of the Board at a hearing in Washington, D.C., at a VA regional office or by videoconference.

The texts of appeal decisions made by the Board, as well as a plain-language pamphlet, "Understanding the Appeal Process," can be found on the Internet (http://www.va.gov/vbs/bva). This pamphlet may also be requested by writing to Chief Bailiff (011), Board of Veterans' Appeals, 810 Vermont Avenue, NW, Washington, DC 20420.

U.S. Court of Appeals for Veterans Claims

A final Board of Veterans' Appeals decision that does not grant a claimant the benefits desired may be appealed to the U.S. Court of Appeals for Veterans Claims, an independent court, not part of the Department of Veterans Affairs.

Notice of an appeal must be received by the court with a postmark that is within 120 days after the date — stamped on the decision — on which the Board of Veterans' Appeals mailed its decision.

The court reviews the record considered by the Board of Veterans' Appeals. It does not hold trials or receive new evidence. Appellants may represent themselves before the court or have lawyers or approved agents as representatives. Oral argument is held only at the direction of the court. Either party may appeal a decision of the court to the U.S. Court of Appeals for the Federal Circuit and may seek review in the Supreme Court of the United States.

The court's Internet website (http://www.vetapp.gov) contains its decisions, case status information, rules and procedures, and other special announcements. The court's decisions can also be found in West's Veterans Appeals Reporter, and on the Westlaw and LEXIS online services. For other questions, write to the Clerk of the Court, 625 Indiana Ave. NW, Suite 900, Washington, DC 20004, or call the clerk's office at 202-501-5970.

2002 Disability Compensation

Disability	Monthly Rate ($)
10 percent	103
20 percent	199
30 percent	306
40 percent	439
50 percent	625
60 percent	790
70 percent	995
80 percent	1,155
90 percent	1,299
100 percent	2,163

Depending upon the disability rating of the veteran, allowances for a spouse range from $37 to $124; and for each additional child, $19 to $64. For more information and detailed disability compensation rate tables, visit the Compensation and Pension Benefits section of VA's Internet pages (http://www.va.gov). Click on "Rate Tables."

2002 Improved Pension

Status	Maximum Annual Rate ($)
Veteran with no dependents	9,556
Veteran with one dependent	12,516
Veteran permanently housebound, no dependents	11,679
Veteran permanently housebound, one dependent	14,639
Veteran needing regular aid and attendance, no dependents	15,945
Veteran needing regular aid and attendance, one dependent	18,902
Two veterans married to one another	12,516
Veterans of World War I and Mexican Border Period, addition to the applicable annual rate	2,166
Increase for each additional dependent child	1,630

Examples and more information can be found in the Compensation and Pension Benefits section of VA's Internet pages (http://www.va.gov). Click on "Rate Tables."

2002 Vocational Rehabilitation Rates
(Paid monthly ($))

Type of training*	No dependent	One dep.	Two dep.	Each add. dep.
A				
Full-time	448.24	556.00	655.20	47.76
3/4-time	336.80	417.61	489.86	36.73
1/2-time	225.36	279.22	328.21	24.50
B				
Full-time	448.24	556.00	655.20	47.76
C				
Full-time	378.65	457.91	527.72	34.32
D				
Full-time	448.24	556.00	655.20	47.76
3/4-time	336.80	417.61	489.86	36.73
1/2-time	225.36	279.22	328.21	24.50
1/4-time	112.66	139.61	164.11	12.23

*Type of training

A. Institutional or independent living training, or unpaid work experience in a federal, state or local agency, or an agency of a federally recognized Indian tribe.

B. Unpaid on-the-job training in a federal, state or local agency, or an agency of a federally recognized Indian tribe; training in a home; vocational course in a rehabilitation facility or sheltered workshop; independent instructor; institutional non-farm cooperative.

C. Farm cooperative, apprenticeship, on-the-job training, or on-the-job non-farm cooperative. VA payment is based on the wage received.

D. Extended evaluation.

Spouses
2002 Dependency and Indemnity Compensation
(Veteran died prior to Jan. 1, 1993)

Pay Grade	Monthly Rate ($)
E-1-E-6	935
E-7	967
E-8	1,021
E-9	1,066
W-1	988
W-2	1,028
W-3	1,058
W-4	1,119
O-1	988
O-2	1,021
O-3	1,092
O-4	1,155
O-5	1,272
O-6	1,433
O-7	1,549
O-8	1,694
O-9	1,818
O-10	1,994

For more information on Dependency and Indemnity Compensation, follow the Compensation and Pension Benefits link on VA's Internet pages (http://www.va.gov). Click on "Rate Tables."

Spouses
2002 Dependency and Indemnity Compensation
(Veteran died on/after Jan. 1, 1993)

Allowances	Monthly Rate ($)
Basic Rate	$935
Additional:	
Each Dependent Child	234
Aid and Attendance	234
Housebound	112
Add $197 if veteran was totally disabled eight continuous years prior to death.	

2002 Improved Death Pension

Recipient	Maximum Annual Rate ($)
Surviving spouse	6,407
With one dependent child	8,389
Surviving spouse permanently housebound	7,832
With dependent child	9,810
Surviving spouse in need of regular aid and attendance	10,243
With dependent child	12,221
Allowance for each additional dependent child	1,630
Pension for each surviving child	1,630

More information on Improved death Pension and Spina Bifida benefits can be found in the Compensation and Pension Benefits section of VA's Internet pages (http://www.va.gov). Click on "Rate Tables."

Spina Bifida Benefits
(Effective Dec. 1, 2001)

	Level I	Level II	Level III
Monthly Rate ($)	228	792	1,354

Provided to children of Vietnam veterans born with spina bifida. The three levels represent degree of disability.

Loan Guaranty Entitlement

Loan Amount	Guaranty Percent	Maximum Amount ($)
Up to $45,000	50	22,500
$45,001 to $56,250	40-50	22,500
$56,251 to $144,000	40	36,000
$144,001 or more	25	60,000
Manufactured home or lot	40	20,000

Funding Fees

Loan Category	Veterans % of loan	Reservists % of loan
Purchase or construction loans with down payments of less than 5 percent, refinancing loans and home improvement loans	2.0	2.75
Purchase or construction loans with down payments of at least 5 percent but less than 10 percent	1.5	2.25
Purchase or construction loans with down payments of 10 percent or more	1.25	2.0
Manufactured home loans	1.0	1.0
Interest rate reduction loans	0.5	0.5
Assumption of VA-guaranteed loans	0.5	0.5
Second or subsequent use without a down payment	3.0	3.0

Important
Phone Numbers

For information on:	Call:
VA Benefits	1-800-827-1000
Health Benefits	1-877-222-8387
Education Benefits	1-888-442-4551
Life Insurance	1-800-669-8477
Debt Management	1-800-827-0648
Mammography Hotline	1-888-492-7844
Telecommunication Device for the Deaf (TDD)	1-800-829-4833
CHAMPVA	1-800-733-8387
Headstones and Markers	1-800-697-6947
Gulf War & Agent Orange Helpline	1-800-749-8387

Health Eligibility Center
1644 Tullie Circle
Atlanta, GA 30329-2303

404-235-1257
or
1-800-929-8387

VA also has a toll-free bulletin board, called VA ONLINE, which can be reached at 1-800-US1-VETS (871-8387).

This VA Federal Benefits booklet and other VA information is available on VA's World Wide Web Home Page at:

http://www.va.gov/

World Wide Web Links

VA home page... http://www.va.gov
VA consumer affairs... http://www.va.gov/customer/conaff.asp
VA public affairs and special events..http://www.va.gov/opa/

VA Benefits and Health Care Information:
VA compensation and pension benefits........................... http://www.vba.va.gov/bln/21/
VA benefits online application.................................http://vabenefits.vba.va.gov/vonapp
Health benefits and services.... ....….. http://www.va.gov/vbs/health/
Burial and memorial benefits.. http://www.cem.va.gov/
Education benefits and services..http://www.gibill.va.gov/
VA home loan guaranties...http://www.homeloans.va.gov/
Board of Veterans' Appeals..http://www.va.gov/vbs/bva
Benefits & services outside the U.S.....................http://www.vba.va.gov/bln/21/foreign/
TRICARE...http://www.tricare.osd.mil/
CHAMPVA..http://www.va.gov/hac/

Forms:
VA forms...http://www.va.gov/forms/
Additional government forms.....................http://www.vba.va.gov/pubs/otherforms.htm

Employment Assistance:
Information for veterans...................................http://www.opm.gov/veterans/index.htm
Veterans' hiring preference ....http://www.opm.gov/veterans/html/vetguide.htm
Federal government job openings......................................http://www.usajobs.opm.gov/
Dept. of Labor Employment & Training Service....................http://www.dol.gov/dol/vets

Business Assistance:
Small Business Administration..http://www.sba.gov/VETS/
Small and Disadvantaged Businesses..... ....http://www.va.gov/OSDBU/

Other useful sites:
Burial in Arlington National Cemetery..................http://www.mdw.army.mil/fs-a02a.htm
Department of Defense...http://www.defenselink.mil/
Military funeral honors.....................................http://www.militaryfuneralhonors.osd.mil/
Military records and medals................................http://www.nara.gov/regional/mpr.html

La versión en español de este folleto.............................http://www.va.gov/opa/feature/

VA Facilities

Note: Patients should call the telephone numbers listed to obtain clinic hours of operation and specialties served.

The following symbols indicate additional programs are available at medical centers:
* for nursing-home care units
# for domiciliaries

ALABAMA
Medical Centers:
Central AL Veterans HC System (1-800-214-8387):
Montgomery 36109 (215 Perry Hill Rd., 334-272-4670)
#*Tuskegee 36083 (2400 Hospital Rd., 334-727-0550)
Birmingham 35233 (700 S. 19th St., 205-933-8101)
*Tuscaloosa 35404 (3701 Loop Rd. East, 205-554-2000)
Clinics:
Anniston 36201 (226 E. 9th St., 256-236-1661)
Anniston 36207 (413 Quintard Ave., 256-231-7980)
Decatur 35601 (401 Lee St. N.E., AM South Bldg., Suite 606, 256-350-1531)
Dothan 36303 (2020 Alexander Dr., 334-272-4670, ext. 4768/4690)
Gadsden 35906 (3004/3006 Rainbow Dr., 256-442-0766/413-7154)
Huntsville 35801 (201 Governor's Dr. S.W., 256-535-1005/1006/1007)
Huntsville 35801 (2006 Franklin St., SE, Suite 104, 256-534-1691)
Jasper 35501 (3400 Hwy 78 East, Medical Towers Suite 215, 205-221-7384)
Mobile 36604 (1504 Springhill Ave., 251-219-3300)
Shoals Area Sheffield 35660 (422DD Cox Blvd., 256-381-3602/9055)

Regional Office:
Montgomery 36109 (345 Perry Hill Rd., statewide, 1-800-827-1000)
Vet Centers:
Birmingham 35233 (1500 5th Ave. South, 205-731-0550)
Mobile 36606 (2577 Government Blvd., 334-478-5906)
National Cemeteries:
Mobile 36604 (1202 Virginia St., for information, call 850-453-4108 or 453-4846)
Fort Mitchell 36856 (Fort Mitchell, 553 Hwy 165, 334-855-4731)

ALASKA
Medical Center:
Alaska Veterans HC System and Regional Office:
Anchorage 99508-2989 (2925 DeBarr Rd, 907-257-4700)
#Homeless Veterans Service:
Anchorage 99503 (3001 C St., 1-800-764-2995)
Clinics:
Kenai 99611 (11355 Frontage Rd., Suite 130, 907-283-2231)
Fairbanks 99703 (Ft. Wainwright, Bassett Army Comm. Hosp., Gaffney Bldg. 4065, Rm. 169/176, 907-353-6370)
Regional Office:
Anchorage 99508-2989 (2925 DeBarr Rd., local, 907-257-5460; statewide, 1-800-827-1000)
Benefits Office:
Juneau 99802 (P.O. Box 20069, 907-586-7472)
Vet Centers:
Anchorage 99508 (4201 Tudor Centre Dr., Suite 115, 907-563-6966)
Fairbanks 99701 (542 4th Ave., Suite 100, 907-456-4238)
Kenai 99669 (Red Diamond Ctr., Bldg. F, Suite 4, 43335 Kalifornsky Beach Rd., 907-260-7640)

Wasilla 99654 (851 E. Westpoint
Ave., Suite 111, 907-376-4318)

National Cemeteries:
Fort Richardson 99505-5498 (Bldg.
#997, Davis Hwy, 907-384-7075)
Sitka 99835 (803 Sawmill Creek
Rd., for information, call 907-384-
7075)

ARIZONA
Medical Centers:
*Phoenix 85012 (650 East Indian
School Rd., 602-277-5551,
Enrollment 602-222-2755)
*#Prescott 86313 (500 Hwy 89
North, 928-445-4860)
*Tucson 85723 (3601 S. 6th Ave.,
520-792-1450)

Clinics:
Bellemont 86015 (Camp Navajo
Army Depot, 520-445-4860 ext.
7820 or 520-226-1056)
Cottonwood 86326 (203 Candy
Lane, Suite 5B, 928-649-1532 or
1-800-949-1005 ext. 7331)
Casa Grande 85222 (Plaza del Sol,
Suites H&I, 900 E. Florence Blvd.,
520-629-4900 or 1-800-470-8262)
Green Valley 85615 (381 W. Vista
Hermonsa, Suite 140, 520-629-
4900 or 1-800-470-8262)
Kingman 86401 (1726 Beverly Ave,
928-445-4860 ext. 6830 or 928-
692-0080)
Lake Havasu City 86403 (2035
Mesquite Ave., Suite E., 520-445-
4860 ext. 7300 or 520-680-0090)
Mesa 85212 (6950 E. Williams Field
Rd., 602-222-2630)
Safford 85546 (Bureau of Land
Management, 711 S. 14'th Ave.,
520-629-4900 or 1-800-470-8262)
Show Low 85901(2450 Show Low
Lake Rd., Suite 1, 520-532-1069)
Sierra Vista 85613 (Ft. Huachuca,
Bliss Army Health Ctr., Bldg.
45001, 520-629-4900 or 1-800-
470-8262)

Sun City 85351 (10147 Grand Ave.,
602-222-2630)
Yuma 85365 (Bureau of Land Mgnt.,
2555 E. Gila Ridge Rd., 520-629-
4900 or 1-800-470-8262)

Regional Office:
Phoenix 85012 (3225 N. Central
Ave.; statewide, 1-800-827-1000)

Vet Centers:
Phoenix 85012 (77 E. Weldon Ave.,
Suite # 100, 602-640-2981)
Prescott 86303 (161 S. Granite St.,
Suite B, 520-778-3469)
Tucson 85719 (3055 N. 1st Ave.,
520-882-0333)

National Cemeteries:
Phoenix 85024 (National Memorial
Cemetery of Arizona, 23029 N.
Cave Creek Rd., 480-513-3600)
Prescott 86301 (500 Hwy 89 N., for
information, call 480-513-3600)

ARKANSAS
Medical Centers:
Fayetteville 72703 (1100 N. College
Ave., 501-443-4301)
Central Arkansas Veterans
Healthcare System:
#*North Little Rock 72114 (2200
Fort Roots Dr., 501-257-1000)
Little Rock 72205 (4300 W. 7th
St., 501-257-1000)

Clinics:
El Dorado 71730 (460 West Oak,
870-881-4426)
Ft. Smith 72901 (Sparks Medical
Plaza, 1500 Dodson Ave., 501
709-6850)
Harrison 72601 (Main St. Clinic, 707
N. Main St., 870 741-3592)
Hot Springs 72214 (1661 Airport
Rd., 501-760-1513)
Jonesboro 72401 (223 East Jack-
son, for information, call Memphis
Med. Ctr., 901-523-8990)
Mountain Home 72653 (405
Buttercup Dr., 870-425-3030)
Paragould 72450 (1101 West
Morgan, Suite #8, 870-236-9756)

Regional Office:
North Little Rock 72115 (Bldg. 65,
Ft. Roots, P.O. Box 1280; state-
wide, 1-800-827-1000)
Vet Center:
North Little Rock 72114 (201 W.
Broadway, Suite A, 501-324-6395)
National Cemeteries:
Fayetteville 72701 (700 Government
Ave., 501-444-5051)
Fort Smith 72901 (522 Garland Ave.,
501-783-5345)
Little Rock 72206 (2523 Confeder-
ate Blvd., 501-324-6401)

CALIFORNIA
Medical Centers:
*Fresno 93703 (2615 E. Clinton
Ave., 559-225-6100)
Greater Los Angeles HC System:
#*West Los Angeles 90073 (11301
Wilshire Blvd., 310-478-3711)
*Loma Linda 92357 (11201 Benton
St., 909-825-7084 or 1-800-741-
8387)
*Long Beach 90822 (5901 E. 7th St.,
562-494-2611)
Northern Calif. HC System:
*Martinez 94553 (150 Muir Rd.,
925-372-2000)
Sacramento 95655 (10535
Hospital Way, 916-366-5366)
Palo Alto HC System:
*Livermore 94550 (4951 Arroyo
Rd., 925-447-2560)
#Menlo Park 94025 (795 Willow
Rd., 650-493-5000)
#*Palo Alto 94304 (3801 Miranda
Ave., 650-493-5000)
San Diego HC System:
*San Diego 92161 (3350 La Jolla
Village Dr., 858-552-8585)
*San Francisco 94121 (4150
Clement St., 415-221-4810)
Clinics:
Anaheim 92801 (1801 W. Romneya
Dr., Suite 303, 714-780-5400)

Antelope Valley/Lancaster 93536
(45120 60th St. West, 661-723-
6373)
Atwater 95301 (3605 Hospital Rd.,
Suite D, 209-381-0105)
Auburn 95603 (3123 Professional
Dr., Suite 250, 1-888-227-5404)
Bakersfield 93301 (1801 Westwind
Dr., 661-632-1800)
Brawley 92227 (528 G. St., 760-344-
1881)
Capitola 95010 (1350 N. 41st St.,
Suite 102, 831-464-5519)
Chico 95926 (280 Cohasset Rd.,
Suite 101, 530-879-5000)
Chula Vista 91910 (835 Third Ave.,
619-409-1600)
Corona 92879 (800 Magnolia Ave,
Suite 101, 909-817-8820)
Culver City 90230 (3831 Hughes
Ave., Suite 104, 310-202-8223)
East Los Angeles 90040 (5426 E.
Olympic Blvd., 323-725-7557)
Escondido 92025 (815 East Penn-
sylvania Ave., 760-745-2000)
Eureka 95501 (727 E. St., 707-442-
5335)
Fairfield 94535 (103 Bodin Circle,
Travis AFB, 707-437-1800)
Gardena 90247 (1251 Redondo
Beach Blvd., 3rd Fl., 310-851-
4705)
Lompoc 93436 (1111 E. Ocean Ave.,
Suite 8, 805-736-7767)
Long Beach 90806 (2001 River Ave.,
562-388-7900)
Los Angeles 90012 (351 E. Temple
St., 213-253-2677)
Mare Island 94592 (Bldg. 201,
Walnut Ave., 707-562-8200)
*Martinez 94553 (150 Muir Rd., 925-
372-2000)
Mission Valley 92108 (8810 Rio San
Diego Dr., 619-400-5000)
Modesto 95350 (1524 McHenry, 3rd
floor, 209-557-6200)
Monterey 93955 (3401 Engineer
Lane, Fort Ord, 831-883-3800)

Oakland 94612 (2221 Martin Luther King Jr. Way, 510-267-7820)

Oakland MHC 94607 (Oakland Army Base, 2505 West 14th St., 510-587-3400)

Oxnard 93030 (250 W. Citrus Grove Ave., 805-983-6384)

Palm Desert 92211 (41865 Board-walk, Suite 103, 760-341-5570 or 800-741-8387)

Redding 96002 (351 Hartnell Ave., 530-226-7500)

Sacramento 95652-1074 (5342 Dudley Blvd., McClellan AFB, 916-561-7400)

San Francisco 94103 (13th & Mission St., Suite 3280, 415-551-7300)

San Jose 95119 (80 Great Oaks Blvd., 408-363-3000)

San Luis Obispo 93401 (1941 Johnson Ave., Suite 202, 805-546-1830)

Santa Ana 92704 (2740 S. Bristol St., Suite 101, 714-825-3500)

Santa Fe Springs 90670 (10210 Orr and Day Rd., 562-864-5565)

Santa Barbara 93110 (4440 Calle Real, 805-683-1491)

Santa Rosa 95403 (3315 Chanate Rd., 707-570-3800)

Seaside 93955 (3401 Engineer Ln., 831-883-3800)

*Sepulveda 91343 (16111 Plummer St., 818-891-7711)

Stockton 95231 (co-located with San Joaquin General Hospital, 500 W. Hospital Rd., 209-468-7040)

Sun City 92586 (28125 Bradley Rd., #130, 909-672-1931 or 800-741-8387)

Tulare 93274 (850 N. Gem St., 559-684-8703)

Ukiah 95482 (238B Hospital Dr., 707-468-1870)

Upland 91786 (1238 E. Arrow Hwy, #100, 909-946-5348)

Victorville 92392 (12138 Industrial Blvd., Suite 120, 760-951-2599 or 800-741-8387)

Vista 92083 (1840 West Dr., 760-643-2000)

Regional Offices:

Los Angeles 90024 (Fed. Bldg., 11000 Wilshire Blvd., serving counties of Inyo, Kern, Los Angeles, Orange, San Bernardino, San Luis Obispo, Santa Barbara and Ventura; statewide, 1-800-827-1000)

San Diego 92108 (8810 Rio San Diego Dr., serving counties of Imperial, Riverside and San Diego; statewide,1-800-827-1000)

Oakland 94612 (1301 Clay St., Rm. 1300 North; statewide, 1-800-827-1000; Recorded benefits, 24-hour availability, 510-637-1325)

Counties of Alpine, Lassen, Modoc and Mono served by Regional Office in Reno, Nev.

Benefits Office:

Commerce 90022-5147 (5400 E. Olympic Blvd., Suite 140, 310-235-6199)

Vet Centers:

Anaheim 92805 (859 S. Harbor Blvd., 714-776-0161)

Chico 95926 (280 Cohasset Rd., 530-899-8549)

Concord 94520 (1899 Clayton Rd., Suite 140, 925-680-4526)

Culver City 90230 (5730 Uplander Way, Suite 100, 310-641-0326)

East Los Angeles 90022 (5400 E. Olympic Blvd., #140, 323-728-9966)

Eureka 95501 (2830 G St., Suite A, 707-444-8271)

Fresno 93726 (3636 N. 1st St., Suite 112, 559-487-5660)

Gardena 90247 (1251 Redondo Beach Blvd., Gardena, 310-767-1221)

Los Angeles 90230 (5730 Uplander Way, Suite 100, Culver City, 310-641-0326)

Marina 93933 (455 Reservation Rd., Suite E, 408-384-1660)

Oakland 94612 (1504 Franklin St., #200, 510-763-3904)

Redwood City 94062 (2946 Broadway St., 650-299-0672)

Riverside 92504 (4954 Arlington Ave., Suite A, 909-359-8967)

Rohnert Park 94928 (6225 State Farm Dr., Suite 101, 707-586-3295)

Sacramento 95825 (1111 Howe Ave., Suite 390, 916-566-7430)

San Bernardino 92408 (155 West Hospitality Lane, Suite #140, 909-890-0797)

San Diego 92103 (2900 6th Ave., 619-294-2040)

San Francisco 94103 (205 13th St., Suite 3190, 415-431-6021)

San Jose 95112 (278 N. 2nd St., 408-993-0729)

Santa Barbara 93101 (1300 Santa Barbara St., 805-564-2345)

Sepulveda 91343 (9737 Haskell Ave., 818-892-9227)

Upland 91786 (313 N. Mountain Ave., 909-982-0416)

Vista 92083 (1830 West Dr., Suite 103, 760-643-2070)

National Cemeteries:

Los Angeles 90049 (950 South Sepulveda Blvd., 310-268-4494)

San Bruno 94066 (Golden Gate, 1300 Sneath Lane, San Francisco Co, call 415-761-1646; San Mateo Co., call 415-589-7737-)

San Diego 92106 (Fort Rosecrans, P.O. Box 6237 Point Loma, 619-553-2084)

Riverside 92518 (22495 Van Buren Blvd., 909-653-8417)

San Francisco 94129 (Presidio of San Francisco, for information, call 415-761-1646)

Gustine 95322 (San Joaquin Valley, 32053 West McCabe Rd., 209-854-1040)

COLORADO

Medical Centers:

*Grand Junction 81501 (2121 North Ave., 970-242-0731)

VA Eastern Colorado HC System Denver 80220 (1055 Claremont St., 303-399-8020)

Pueblo 81005 (1339 S. Pueblo Blvd., 719-566-6193)

Clinics:

Alamosa, CO 81101 (1847 2nd St., 719-589-4488/4494)

Aurora 80045 (13001 East 17th Place, Bldg. 500, 2nd floor, 303-724-0190)

Colorado Springs 80905 (25 N. Spruce St., 719-327-5660))

Fort Collins 80524 (1100 Poudre River Dr., 970-224-1550)

Greeley 80631 (2020 16th St., 970-313-0027)

LaJunta 81050 (1100 Carson Ave., Suite 104, 719-383-5195)

Lakewood 80225 (155 Van Gordon St., Suite 395, 303-914-2680)

Lamar 81052 (301 Kendall Dr., 719-336-5972)

Montrose 81401 (4 Hillcrest Plaza Way, 970-249-7791)

Pueblo, CO 81008 (4112 Outlook Blvd., 719-553-1000)

Regional Office:

Denver 80225 (Box 25126; statewide, 1-800-827-1000)

Vet Centers:

Boulder 80302 (2336 Canyon Blvd., Suite 130, 303-440-7306)

Colorado Springs 80903 (416 E. Colorado Ave., 719-471-9992)

Denver 80220 (7465 E. Academy Blvd., Suite B, 303-326-0645)

National Cemeteries:

Denver 80235 (Fort Logan, 3698 S. Sheridan Blvd., 303-761-0117)

Fort Lyon 81038 (for information, call, 303-761-0117)

CONNECTICUT
Medical Centers:
Conn. HC System:
 *West Haven Division 06516 (950 Campbell Ave., 203-932-5711)
 Newington Division 06111 (555 Willard Ave., 860-666-6951)
Clinics:
Stamford 06904 (128 Strawberry Hill Ave., 1-888-844-4441)
New London 06320 (15 Mohegan Ave., 860-437-3611)
Waterbury 06706 (133 Scovill St.; 203-465-5292)
Windham 06226 (96 Mansfield St., 860-450-7583)
Winsted 06098 (115 Spencer St., 860-738-6985)
Regional Office:
Hartford 06103 (450 Main St.; statewide, 1-800-827-1000)
Vet Centers:
New Haven 06516 (141 Captain Thomas Blvd., 203-932-9899)
Norwich 06360 (60 Main St., 860-887-1755)
Wethersfield 06109 (30 Jordan Lane, 860-240-3543)

DELAWARE
Medical Center:
 *Wilmington 19805 (1601 Kirkwood Hwy, 302-994-2511)
Clinic:
Millsboro 19966 (214 W. DuPont Hwy, 302-633-5212)
Regional Office:
Wilmington 19805 (1601 Kirkwood Hwy, statewide, 1-800-827-1000)
Vet Center:
Wilmington 19805 (1601 Kirkwood Hwy, Bldg. 3, 302-994-1660)

DISTRICT OF COLUMBIA:
Medical Center:
 *Washington, D.C. 20422 (50 Irving St., N.W., 202-745-8000)
Clinic:
Southeast 20032 (820 Chesapeake St., S.E., 202-745-8685)
Regional Office:
Washington, D.C. 20421 (1120 Vermont Ave., N.W., local, 1-800-827-1000)
Vet Center:
Washington, D.C. 20032 (911 2nd St., N.E., 202-543-8821)

FLORIDA
Medical Centers:
#*Bay Pines 33744 (10000 Bay Pines Blvd., N., 727-398-6661)
N. Florida/S. Georgia Veterans HC System:
 *Gainesville 32608 (1601 Southwest Archer Rd., 352-376-1611)
 *Lake City 32025 (801 S. Marion St., 386-755-3016)
 *Miami 33125 (1201 N.W. 16th St., 305-324-4455)
 *Tampa 33612 (13000 Bruce B. Downs Blvd., 813-972-2000)
 *West Palm Beach 33410 (7305 N. Military Trail, 561-882-8262)
Clinics:
Boca Raton 33431 (900 Glades Rd., 561 416-8995)
Brevard 32940 (2900 Veterans Way, Viera, 321-637-3788)
Brooksville 34613 (14540 Cortez Blvd., Suite 202, 352-597-8287)
Clearwater 33719 (Oak Brook Plaza, 2465 McMullen Booth Rd. 727-797-3789)
Coral Springs 33065 (9900 West Sample Rd., Suite 100, 954-575-4940)
Daytona Beach 32114 (551 National Health Care Dr., 904-274-4600)
Deerfield Beach 33442 (2100 SW 10th St., 954-570-5572)

Delray Beach 33445 (4800 Linton Blvd, 561-495-1973)

Ellenton, 34222 (4333 U.S. 301 North, 941-721-0649)

Fort Myers 33916 (3033 Winkler Ext.ension, 941-939-3939)

Ft. Pierce 34950 (728 North US 1, 561-595-5150)

Hallandale 33009 (2500 E. Hallandale Beach Blvd., Penthouse II, 954-454-7788)

Homestead 33030 (950 Krome Ave., Suite 401, 305-248-0874)

Inverness 34104 (Citrus Co., 401 Central Ave., 352 637-3500)

Jacksonville 32206 (1833 Blvd., 904-232-2712)

Key Largo 33037 (105662 Overseas Hwy, 305-451-0164)

Key West 33040 (1300 Douglas Cir., 305-293-4609)

Kissimmee 34741 (201 Hilda St., 407-518-5004)

Lakeland 33803 (3240 S. Florida Ave., Lakeland, 863-701-2474)

Leesburg 34788 (9836 S. Hwy 441, Leesburg, 352-728-4462)

Manatee 34222 (4333 U.S. Hwy 301 North, 941-721-0649)

Naples (Collier Co.) 34104 (2685 Horseshoe Dr., S., 941-659-9188)

N. Pinellas County 34619 (2465 McMullen-Booth Rd., 727-797-3789)

Oakland Park 33334 (5599 N. Dixie Hwy, 954-771-2101)

Ocala 34470 (1515 E. Silver Springs Blvd., 352-369-3320)

Okeechobee 34971 (1201 N. Parrott Ave., 863 824-3232)

Orlando 32803 (5201 Raymond St., 407-629-1599)

Panama City 32407 (6703 West Hwy 98, Bldg. 387, 850-235-5101)

Pembroke Pines 33024 (7369 Sherdian St., 954-894-1668)

Pensacola 32503 (312 Kenmore Rd., 850-476-1100)

Port Charlotte 33952 (2885 Tamiami Trail, Suite 301, 941-235-2710)

Port Richey 34652 (9912 Little Rd., 727-869-4100)

Sanford 32771 (209 San Carlos Ave., 407-323-5999)

Sarasota 34233 (4000 Sawyer Rd., 941-927-8422)

South St. Petersburg 33711 (3420 8th Ave. South, 727-322-1304)

St. Augustine 32806 (1955 US 1 South, 904 829-0814)

Stuart 34994 (618 SE Ocean Blvd., 561-288-0304)

Tallahassee 32308 (1607 St. James Ct., 850-878-0191)

Vero Beach 32961 (1485 37th St., Suite 102, 561 299-4623)

Zephyrhills 33541 (37814 Medical Arts Ct., 813-780-2550)

Regional Office:

St. Petersburg 33731 (9500 Bay Pines Blvd., 1-800-827-1000)

Benefits Offices:

Fort Myers 33916 (3033 Winkler Ave., Ext., 941-939-3939)

Jacksonville 32206 (1833 Blvd., Rm. 3109, 1-800-827-1000)

Miami 33130 (Fed. Bldg., Rm. 120, 51 S.W. 1st Ave., 1-800-827-1000)

Oakland Park 33334 (5599 North Dixie Hwy, 1-800-827-1000)

Pensacola 32503-7492 (312 Kenmore Rd., Rm. 1G250, 1-800-827-1000)

Vet Centers:

Ft. Lauderdale 33304 (713 N.E. 3rd Ave., 954-356-7926)

Jacksonville 32202 (300 East State St., 904-232-3621)

Miami 33129 (2700 S.W. 3rd Ave., Suite1A, 305-859-8387)

Orlando 32822 (5575 S. Semoran Blvd., Suite 36, 407-857-2800)

Palm Beach 33461 (2311 10th Ave., North #13, 561-585-0441)

Pensacola 32501 (202 W. Jackson St., 850-435-8761)

Sarasota 34231 (4801 Swift Rd., 941-927-8285)
St. Petersburg 33713 (2837 1st Ave., N., 727-893-3791)
Tallahassee 32303 (249 E. 6th Ave., 850-942-8810)
Tampa 33604 (1507 W. Sligh Ave., 727-228-2621)

National Cemeteries:
Barrancas 32508-1099 (80 Hovey Rd., Naval Air Station Pensacola, 850-453-4108 or 850-453-4846)
Bay Pines 33504-0477 (10000 Bay Pines Blvd., North, for information, call 727-398-9426)
Bushnell 33513 (6502 SW 102nd Ave., 352-793-7740 or 352-793-1074)
St. Augustine 32084 (104 Marine St., for information, call 352-793-7740)

GEORGIA
Medical Centers:
*Augusta 30904 (1 Freedom Way, 706-733-0188)
*Decatur 30033 (1670 Clairmont Rd., 404-321-6111)
#*Dublin 31021 (1826 Veterans Blvd., 478-272-1210 or 1-800-595-5229)

Clinics:
Albany 31701 (521 Third Ave., 229-446-9000 or 1-800-341-5751)
Atlanta 30309 (77 Peachtree Place, 404-321-6111, ext. 2600)
Columbus 31906 (Medical Arts Bldg, 1310 13th Ave., 706-257-7200, 334-727-0550, ext. 3959/4135)
Lawrenceville 30043 (1970 River-side Pkwy., 404-417-1750)
Macon 31210 (140 North Crest Blvd., 478-476-8868)
Northeast Georgia 30566 (3931 Munday Mill Rd., 404-728-8210)
Savannah 31406 (325 W. Montgomery CrossRd., 912-920-0214)
Valdosta 31601 (3123 North Ashley St., 912-283-0132)

West Marietta/Cobb 30064 (1225 Powder Spring Rd., 770-803-6646)
Regional Office:
Decatur 30333 (1700 Clairmont Rd., statewide, 1-800-827-1000)
Vet Centers:
Atlanta 30309 (77 Peachtree Pl., N.W., 404-347-7264)
Savannah 31406 (8110A White Bluff Rd., 912-652-4097)
National Cemetery:
Marietta 30060 (500 Washington Ave., for information, call 334-855-4731)

GUAM
Clinic:
Agana Heights 96919 (U.S. Naval Hospital, 313 Farenholt Rd., 671-344-9200)
Vet Center:
Agana 96910 (222 Chalan Santo Papa St., Reflection Center, Suite 102, 671-472-7160 or 7161)

HAWAII
Medical & Regional Office:
Honolulu 96813 (300 Ala Moana Blvd.; Medical & Regional Office, 808-566-1409; toll-free from Hawaiian neighbor islands, 1-800-827-1000; toll-free from American Samoa, 11-877-285-1128; toll-free from Guam, 475-8387; toll-free from Saipan, Rota, & Tinian, 1-888-253-2750)
Vet Centers:
Hilo 96720 (120 Keawe St., Suite 201, 808-969-3833)
Honolulu 96814 (1680 Kapiolani Blvd., Suite F.3, 808-969-3833)
Kailua-Kona 96740 (Pottery Terrace, Fern Bldg., 75-5995 Kuakini Hwy, # 415, 808-329-0574)
Lihue 96766 (3367 Kuhio Hwy, Suite 101, 808-246-1163)
Wailuku 96793 (35 Lunalilo, Suite 101, 808-242-8557)

National Cemetery:
Honolulu 96813-1729 (National
Memorial Cemetery of the Pacific,
2177 Puowaina Dr., 808-532-
3720)

IDAHO
Medical Center:
*Boise 83702 (500 West Fort St.,
208-422-1000)
Clinics:
Pocatello 83201 (1651 Alvin Ricken
Dr., 208-232-6214)
Twin Falls 83301 (260 2nd Ave, E.,
208-732-0947)
Regional Office:
Boise 83702 (805 W. Franklin St.;
statewide, 1-800-827-1000)
Vet Centers:
Boise 83705 (5440 Franklin Rd.,
Suite 100, 208-342-3612)
Pocatello 83201 (1800 Garrett Way,
208-232-0316)

ILLINOIS
Medical Centers:
Chicago HC System
Lakeside Division 60611 (333 E.
Huron St., 312-569-8387)
Westside Division 60612 (820 S.
Damen Ave., 312-569-8387)
* VA Illiana Health Care System
61832 (Danville Med. Ctr., 1900 E.
Main St., 217-442-8000 or 800-
320-8387)
*Hines 60141 (Roosevelt Rd. & 5th
Ave., 708-202-8387)
*Marion 62959 (2401 W. Main St.,
618-997-5311)
#*North Chicago 60064 (3001 Green
Bay Rd., 847-688-1900)
Clinics:
Aurora 60506 (1700 N. Landmark
Rd., 630-859-2504)
Belleville 62223 (29 N. 64th St., 618-
398-2100)
Chicago 60643 (2038 W. 95th St.,
773-363-5748)

Decatur 62526 (3035 E. Mound Rd.,
217-875-2670 or 800-320-8387)
Effingham 62401 (301 W. Virginia,
217-347-7600)
Elgin 60123 (1231 N. Larkin Blvd.,
847-742-5920)
Evanston 60202 (107 -109 Clyde
St., 847-869-6315)
Galesburg 61401 (695 N. Kellogg
St, 309-343-0311)
Joliet 60435 (2000 Glenwood Ave.,
815-223-9678)
Lafayette 47906 (3851 N. River Rd.,
765-464-2280)
LaSalle 61301 (2970 Chartres St.,
815-223-9678)
Manteno 60950 (One Veterans Dr.,
815-468-1027)
McHenry 60050 (620 S. Route 31,
815-759-2306)
Mt. Vernon 62864, (#1 Doctors Park
Rd., 618-246-2910 or 2911)
Oak Park 60302 (149 S. Oak Park
Ave., 708-386-3008)
Peoria 61605 (411 Martin Luther
King Jr. Dr., 309-671-7350 or 800-
320-8387)
Quincy 62301 (1707 North 12th St.,
217-224-3366)
Rockford 61108 (4940 East State
St., 815-227-0081)
Springfield 62701 (326 N. 7th St.,
217-522-9730 or 800-320-8387)
Regional Office:
Chicago 60605 (536 S. Clark St.,
P.O. Box 8136; statewide, 1-800-
827-1000)
Vet Centers:
Chicago 60637 (1514 E. 63rd. St.,
773-684-5500)
Chicago Heights 60411 (1600
Halsted St., 708-754-0340)
East St. Louis 62203 (1269 N. 89th
St., Suite 1, 618-397-6602)
Evanston 60202 (565 Howard St.,
847-332-1019)
Moline 61265 (1529 46th Ave., # 6,
309-762-6954)

Oak Park 60302 (155 S. Oak Park
Blvd., 708-383-3225)
Peoria 61603 (3310 N. Prospect
Rd., 309-671-7300)
Springfield 62702 (624 S. 4th St.,
217-492-4955)
National Cemeteries:
Alton 62003 (600 Pearl St., for
information, call 314-260-8720)
Danville 61832 (1900 East Main St.,
217-554-4550)
Elwood 60421 (Abraham Lincoln,
27034 S. Diagonal Rd., 815-423-
9958)
Mound City 62963 (Junction Hwy 37
& 51, for information, call 314-
260-8720)
Quincy 62301 (36th and Maine St.,
for information, call 309-782-2094)
Rock Island 61299-7090 (Rock
Island Arsenal, Bldg. 118, 309-
782-2094)
Springfield 62707 (Camp Butler,
5063 Camp Butler Rd., 217-492-
4070)

INDIANA
Medical Centers:
Indianapolis 46202 (1481 W. 10th
St., 317-554-0000)
Northern Indiana HC System:
*Fort Wayne 46805 (2121 Lake
Ave., 219-426-5431)
*Marion 46953 (1700 E. 38th St.,
765-674-3321)
Clinics:
Bloomington 47401 (200 E. Winslow
Rd., 812-353-2600)
Crown Point 46307 (9330 S.
Broadway, 219-662-0001)
Evansville 47713 (500 E. Walnut,
812-465-6202)
Lawrenceburg 47025 (710 W. Eads
Pkwy, 812-539-2313)
Muncie/Anderson 47304 (3500 W.
Purdue Ave., 765-284-6860)
New Albany 47150 (811 Northgate
Blvd., 502-894-6188)

Richmond 47346 (4351 South A St.,
765-973-6915)
South Bend 46635 (17615 State Rd.
23, 219-251-2819)
Terre Haute 47804 (1635 North
Third St., 812-232-2890)
West Lafayette 47906 (3851 N.
River Rd., 765-464-2280 or 800-
320-8387)
Regional Office:
Indianapolis 46204 (575 N. Pennsyl-
vania St.; statewide, 1-800-827-
1000)
Vet Centers:
Evansville 47711 (311 N. Weinbach
Ave., 812-473-5993 or 473-6084)
Fort Wayne 46802 (528 West Berry
St., 219-460-1456)
Highland 46322 (9105A Indianapolis
Blvd., Suite 301, 219-923-2871)
Indianapolis 46208 (3833 N. Meri-
dian, Suite 120, 317-927-6440)
National Cemeteries:
Indianapolis 46208 (Crown Hill, 700
W. 38th St., for information, call
765-674-0284)
Marion 46952 (1700 E. 38th St.,
765-674-0284)
New Albany 47150 (1943 Ekin Ave.,
for information, call 502-893-3852)

IOWA
Medical Centers:
Central Iowa HC System:
#Des Moines 50310 (3600 30th
St., 800-294-8387)
#*Knoxville 50138 (1515 W.
Pleasant St., 800-816-8878)
Iowa City 52246 (601 Hwy 6 West,
319-338-0581)
Clinics:
Bettendorf 52722 (2979 Victoria St.,
319-332-8528)
Dubuque 52001 (250 Mercy Dr.,
319-589-8899)
Fort Dodge 50501 (804 Kenyon Rd.,
Suite 160, 515-576-2235 or 877-
578-8846)

Mason City 50401 (910 N. Eisenhower, 641-421-8077 or 800-351-4671)
Sioux City 51104 (1551 Indian Hills Dr., Suite 206, 712-258-4700)
Waterloo 50703 (2055 Kimball Ave, Suite 320, 319-272-2424)
Regional Office:
Des Moines 50309 (210 Walnut St., Rm. 1063; statewide, 1-800-827-1000)
Vet Centers:
Cedar Rapids 52402 (1642 42nd St. N.E., 319-378-0016)
Des Moines 50310 (2600 M. L. King Jr. Pkwy., 515-284-4929)
Sioux City 51104 (1551 Indian Hills Dr., 712-255-3808)
National Cemetery:
Keokuk 52632 (1701 J St., for information, call 309-782-2094)

KANSAS
Medical Centers:
Eastern Kansas HC System:
#*Leavenworth 66048 (4101 S. 4th St., Trafficway,913-682-2000)
*Topeka 66622 (2200 SW Gage Blvd., 785-350-3111)
*Wichita 67218 (5500 E. Kellogg, 316-685-2221)
Clinics:
Abilene 67410 (510 NE 10th St., 785-263-2100, ext. 161)
Chanute 66720 (629 S. Plummer, 316-431-4000, ext. 1553)
Dodge City 67801 (300 Custer, 620-225-7146)
Emporia 66801 (12th and Chestnut, 316-434-6800, ext. 3351)
Fort Riley 66442 (Bldg. 600, 1st Fl., Huebner Rd. 785-239-7720)
Fort Scott 66701 (710 W. 8th St., 316-223-8400)
Garnett 66032 (421 S. Maple, 785-448-3131, ext. 309)
Hays 67601 (207B E. 7th St.,, 785-625-3550)

Holton 66436 (1110 Columbine Dr., 785-364-2116, ext. 115)
Junction City 66441 (1102 St. Mary's Rd., 785-238-4131, ext. 4408)
Kansas City 66102 (21 N. 12th St., Suite 200, 800-952-8387, ext. 6990)
Lawrence 66044 (404 Maine St., 785-842-3635)
Liberal 67901 (2130 N. Kansas Ave., 316-626-5574)
Paola 66071 (501 S. Hospital Dr., Suite 100, 816-922-2160 or 913-294-4765)
Parsons 67357 (1401 Main, 316-423-3858)
Russell 67665 (200 South Main St., 785-483-3131, ext. 378)
Salem 65560 (Hwy 72 North, 573-729-6626)
Seneca 66538 (1600 Community Dr., 785-336-6181, ext. 162)
Regional Office:
Wichita 67218 (5500 E. Kellogg, 1-800-827-1000)
Vet Center:
Wichita 67211 (413 S. Pattie, 316-265-3260)
National Cemeteries:
Fort Leavenworth 66027 (for information, call 913-758-4105)
Fort Scott 66701 (900 East National, 316-223-2840)
Leavenworth 66048 (P.O. Box 1694, 913-758-4105)

KENTUCKY
Medical Centers:
#* Ft. Thomas 41075 (1000 S. Ft. Thomas Ave., 513-861-3100)
*Lexington 40502-2236 (1101 Veterans Dr., 859-233-4511)
Louisville 40206 (800 Zorn Ave., 502-895-3401)
Clinics:
Bellevue 41073 (103 Landmark Dr., 859-392-3840)
Fort Campbell 42223 (Desert Storm Ave., Bldg. 61639, 270-798-4118)

Fort Knox 40121 (851 Ireland Ave., 502-624-9396)
Louisville; Dupont 40207 (4010 Dupont Circle, 502-894-6187)
Louisville; Shively 40216 (3934 N. Dixie Hwy, Suite 210, 502-449-6986)
Paducah 42001 (1800 Clark St., 270-444-8465)
Prestonsburg 41602 (Riverview Professional Ctr., 606-886-1970)
Somerset 42501 (104 Hardin Lane, 606-676-0786)
Whitesburg 41858 (226 Medical Plaza Lane, 606-633-4871)

Regional Office:
Louisville 40202 (545 S. Third St.; statewide, 1-800-827-1000)

Vet Centers:
Lexington 40507 (301 E. Vine St., Suite C, 859-253-0717)
Louisville 40208 (1347 S. 3rd St., 502-634-1916)

National Cemeteries:
Danville 40442 (277 N. First St., for information, call 859-885-5727)
Lebanon 40033 (20 Hwy 208, call 502-893-3852)
Lexington 40508 (833 W. Main St., for information, call 859-885-5727)
Louisville 40204 (Cave Hill, 701 Baxter Ave., for information, call 502-893-3852)
Louisville 40207 (Zachary Taylor, 4701 Brownsboro Rd., 502-893-3852)
Nancy 42544 (Mill Springs, 9044 West Hwy 80, for information, call 859-885-5727)
Nicholasville 40356 (Camp Nelson, 6980 Danville Rd., 859-885-5727)

LOUISIANA
Medical Centers:
*Alexandria 71306 (2495 Shreveport Hwy 71 North, Pineville, 318-473-0010)
*New Orleans 70112 (1601 Perdido St., 504-568-0811)

Shreveport 71101 (510 E. Stoner Ave., 318-221-8411)

Clinics:
Baton Rouge 70806 (216 S. Foster Dr., 225-925-3099)
Jennings 70546 (1907 Johnson St., 337-824-1000)
Monroe 71203 (250 DeSiard Plaza, 318-343-6100)
Lafayette 70510 (2100 Jefferson St. 337-261-0734

Regional Office:
New Orleans 70113 (701 Loyola Ave., Rm. 4210, statewide, 1-800-827-1000)

Vet Centers:
New Orleans 70116 (1533 N. Claiborne Ave., 504-943-8386)
Shreveport 71104 (2800 Youree Dr., Bldg. 1, Suite 105, 318-861-1776)

National Cemeteries:
Baton Rouge 70806 (220 N. 19th St., for information, call 225-654-3767)
Pineville 71360 (Alexandria, 209 E. Shamrock St., for information, call 601-445-4981)
Zachary 70791 (Port Hudson, 20978 Port Hickey Rd., 225-654-3767)

MAINE
Medical Center:
*Togus 04330 (1 VA Center, 207-623-8411)

Regional Office:
Togus 04330 (1 VA Center, state-wide, 1-800-827-1000)

Clinics:
Bangor 04401 (304 Hancock St., Suite 3B, 207-941-8160)
Calais 04619 (1 Palmer St., 207-454-7849)
Caribou 04736 (163 Van Buren Rd., Suite 6, 207-498-8785)
Rumford 04276 (209 Lincoln Ave., 207-364-4048)
Saco 04072 (53 Beach St., 207-282-4700)

Vet Centers:
Bangor 04401 (352 Harlow St., 207-947-3391)
Caribou 04736 (456 York St., Irving Complex, 207-496-3900)
Lewiston 04240 (Pkwy Complex, 29 Westminster St., 207-783-0068)
Portland 04103 (475 Stevens Ave., 207-780-3584)
Springvale 04083 (628 Main St., 207-490-1513)
National Cemetery:
Togus 04330 (VA Medical and Regional Office Center, for information, call 508-563-7113)

MARYLAND
Medical Centers:
Maryland HC System:
*Baltimore 21201 (10 N. Green St., 410-605-7000)
Fort Howard 21052 (9600 N. Point Rd., 410-477-1800)
#Perry Point 21902 (Circle Dr., 410-642-2411)
Baltimore 21201 (Prosthetic Assessment Information Ctr.,103 S. Gay St., 410-962-3934)
Baltimore 21218 (Rehabilitation and Extended Care Ctr., 3900 Loch Raven Blvd., 410-605-7508)
Clinics:
Cambridge 21613 (830 Chesapeake Dr., 410-228-6243)
Charlotte Hall 20622 (29431 Charlotte Hall Rd., 310-884-7102)
Cumberland 21502 (710 Memorial Ave., 301-724-0061)
Glen Burnie 21061 (1406 South Crain Hwy, 410-590-4140)
Greenbelt 20770 (7525 Greenway Ctr. Dr., Suite T-4, 301-345-2463)
Hagerstown 21742 (1101 Opal Court, 301-665-1462)
Loch Raven 21218 (3901 The Alameda, 410-605-7650)
Pocomoke 21851 (101B Market St., 410-957-6718)

Regional Office:
Baltimore 21201 (31 Hopkins Plaza Federal Bldg., I-800-827-1000; counties of Montgomery and Prince Georges served by Washington, DC, RO, 1-800-827-1000)
Vet Centers:
Baltimore 21207 (6666 Security Blvd., Suite 2, 410-277-3600)
Cambridge 21613 (5510 West Shore Dr., 410-228-6305 ext. 4123)
Elkton 21921 (103 Chesapeake Blvd. Suite A, 410-394-4485)
Silver Spring 20910 (1015 Spring St., Suite 101, 301-589-1073)
National Cemeteries:
Annapolis 21401 (800 West St., for information, call 410-644-9696)
Baltimore 21228 (5501 Frederick Ave., 410-644-9696)
Loudon Park 21228 (Baltimore, 3445 Frederick Ave., for information, call 410-644-9696)

MASSACHUSETTS
Medical Centers:
Bedford 01730 (200 Springs Rd., 1-800-838-6331 or 781-275-7500)
Boston 02130 (150 S. Huntington Ave., 617-232-9500)
Brockton 02301 (940 Belmont St., 508-583-4500)
*Northampton 01053-9764 (421 N. Main St., 413-584-4040)
West Roxbury 02132 (1400 VFW Pkwy., 617-323-7700)
Clinics:
Boston 02114 (251 Causeway St., 617-248-1000)
Dorchester 02124 (895 Blue Hill Ave., 617-822-0381
Edgartown 02539 (55 Simpson's Lane, 508-627-1044)
Fitchburg 01420 (275 Nichols Rd., 978-342-9781)
Framingham 01702 (61 Lincoln St., 508-628-0205)

Gloucester 01930 (298 Washington St., 978-282-0676)
Greenfield 01301 (51 Sanderson St., Suite 9, 413-773-8428)
Haverhill 01830 (108 Merrimack St., 978-372-5207)
Hyannis 02601 (145 Falmouth Rd., 508-771-3190)
Lowell 01852 (130 Marshall Rd., 978-671-9000)
Lynn 01904 (225 Boston St., Suite 107, 781-595-9818)
Nantucket 02554 (57 Prospect St., 508-825-8200)
New Bedford 02740 (175 Elm St., 508-994-0217)
Pittsfield 01201 (73 Eagle St., 413-443-4857)
Quincy 02169 (114 Whitwell St., 2nd Floor, 617-376-2010)
Springfield 01103 (1550 Main St., 413-785-0301)
Worcester 01605 (605 Lincoln St., 508-856-0104)

Regional Office:
Boston 02203 (JFK Fed. Bldg., Gov. Ctr., Rm. 1265; statewide, 1-800-827-1000)
(Towns of Fall River & New Bedford, counties of Barnstable, Dukes, Nantucket, Bristol, part of Plymouth served by Providence, R.I., Regional Office)

Vet Centers:
Boston 02215 (665 Beacon St., 617-424-0665)
Brockton 02401 (1041-L Pearl St., 508-580-2730)
Lowell 01852 (73 East Merrimack St., 978-453-1151)
New Bedford 02740 (468 North St., 508-999-6920)
Springfield 01103 (1985 Main St., Northgate Plaza, 413-737-5167)
Worcester 01605 (597 Lincoln St., 508-856-7428)

National Cemetery:
Bourne 02532 (Massachusetts, Connery Ave., 508-563-7113)

MICHIGAN
Medical Centers:
*Ann Arbor 48105 (2215 Fuller Rd., 734-769-7100)
*Battle Creek 49016 (5500 Armstrong Rd., 616-966-5600)
*Detroit 48201 (4646 John R. St., 313-576-1000)
*Iron Mountain 49801 (325 E. H St., 906-774-3300 or 1-800-215-8262 in Mich. and Wis.)
*Saginaw 48602 (1500 Weiss St., 989-497-2500)

Clinics:
Flint 48532 (G-3267 Beecher Rd., 810-720-2913)
Gaylord 49735 (806 S. Otsego, 989-732-6555)
Grand Rapids 49505 (3019 Coit, N.E., 616-365-9575)
Hancock 49930-1495 (890 Campus Dr., 906-482-7762)
Ironwood 49938 (Grandview Rd.,906-932-1500)
Jackson 49202 (2200 Springport Rd., 517-787-8010)
Lansing 48910 (2727 S. Pennsylvania, 517-374-4295)
Marquette 49855 (425 Fisher St., 906-226-4618)
Menominee 49858 (1101 11th Ave., Suite 2, 906-863-1286)
Muskegon 49442 (165 E. Apple Ave., 616-725-4105)
Oscoda 48750 (5671 Skeel Ave., Suite 4., 989-747-0026)
Pontiac 48342 (950 University Dr., 248-338-5648)
Sault Ste. Marie 49783 (2864 Ashmun Rd., 906-253-9564)
Traverse City 49648 (745 S. Garfield, 231-932-9720)
Yale 48097 (7470 Brockway Rd., 810-387-3211)

Regional Office:
Detroit 48226 (Patrick V. McNamara Fed. Bldg., 477 Michigan Ave., Rm. 1400; statewide,1-800-827-1000)
Vet Centers:
Benton Harbor 49022 (906 Agard Ave., 616-925-5912)
Dearborn 48124-3438 (2811 Monrow St., 313-277-1428)
Detroit 48201 (4161 Cass Ave., 313-831-6509)
Grand Rapids 49507 (1940 Eastern SE, 616-243-0385)
National Cemetery:
Augusta 49012 (Fort Custer, 15501 Dickman Rd., 616-731-4164)

MINNESOTA
Medical Centers:
*Minneapolis 55417 (One Veterans Dr., 612-725-2000)
#*St. Cloud 56303 (4801 8th St. N., 320-252-1670 or 1-800-247-1739)
Clinics:
Brainerd 56401 (1777 Hwy 18 East, 218-855-1115)
Fergus Falls 56537 (1821 North Park St., 218-739-1400)
Hibbing Area, 4 sites (for information, call 612-725-1991)
Mankato Area, 24 sites (for information, call 612-725-1991)
Maplewood 55109 (2785 White Bear Ave., Suite 210, 651-290-3040)
Regional Office and Ins.Center:
St. Paul 55111 (Bishop Henry Whipple Federal Bldg., 1 Federal Dr., Fort Snelling; statewide, 1-800-827-1000)
(Counties of Becker, Beltrami, Clay, Clearwater, Kittson, Lake of the Woods, Mahnomen, Marshall, Norman, Otter Tail, Pennington, Polk, Red Lake, Roseau, Wilkin served by Fargo, N.D., Regional Office)

Vet Centers:
Duluth 55802 (405 E. Superior St., 218-722-8654)
St. Paul 55114 (2480 University Ave., 651-644-4022)
National Cemetery:
Minneapolis 55450-1199 (Fort Snelling, 7601 34th Ave. So.,612-726-1127)

MISSISSIPPI
Medical Centers:
#*Biloxi 39531 (400 Veterans Ave., 228-523-5000)
*Jackson 39216 (1500 E. Woodrow Wilson Dr., 601-362-4471)
Clinics:
Byhalia 38611 (12 East Brunswick St., for information, call Memphis Med. Ctr., 901-523-8990)
Greenville 38703 (1502 S. Colorado St., 662-332-9872)
Hattiesburg 39401 (231 Methodist Blvd., 601-296-3530)
Koscuisko 39090 (332 Hwy 12 W., 662-289-5790, ext. 3039)
Meridian 39301 (2103 13th St., 601-482-3275)
Natchez 39120 (46 Sgt. Prentiss Dr., 601-384-8207)
Smithville 38870 3 sites (63420 Hwy 25 North, for information, call Memphis Med. Ctr., 901-523-8990)
Regional Office:
Jackson 39216 (1600 E. Woodrow Wilson Ave., 1-800-827-1000)
Vet Centers:
Biloxi 39531 (313 Abbey Ct., 228-388-9938 or 228-388-6923)
Jackson 39206 (4436 N. State St., Suite A3, 601-965-5727)
National Cemeteries:
Biloxi 39535-4968 (P.O. Box 4968, 228-388-6668)
Corinth 38834 (1551 Horton St., for information, call 901-386-8311)
Natchez 39120 (41 Cemetery Rd., 601-445-4981)

MISSOURI
Medical Centers:
*Columbia 65201 (800 Hospital Dr., 573-814-6000)

Kansas City 64128 (4801 Linwood Blvd., 816-861-4700)

*Poplar Bluff 63901 (1500 N. Westwood Blvd., 573-686-4151)

St. Louis 63106 (915 N. Grand Blvd., 314-652-4100)

*St. Louis 63125 (#1 Jefferson Barracks Dr., 314-487-0400)

Clinics:
Belton 64012 (17140 Bel-Ray Place, 816-922-2161 or 816-318-0251)

Cape Girardeau 63701 (1923 N. Kings Hwy, 573-339-0909)

Camdenton 65020 (RR 2, 573-346-5624)

Farmington 63640 (715 Maple Valley Dr., 573-760-1365)

Ft. Leonard Wood 65473 (126 Missouri Ave., 573-329-8305)

Kirksville 63501 (1108 East Patterson, Suite 9, 660-627-8387)

Lake Ozark 65049 (1870 Bagnell Dam Blvd., 573-365-2318)

Mt. Vernon 65712 (600 N. Main St., 417-466-4000)

Nevada 64772, (322 Prewitt, 417-448-8905)

Osage Beach 65065 (Lake of the Ozarks, 573-365-2318)

St. Charles 63304, (#7 Jason Court, 636-498-1113)

St. Joseph 64506 (1011B East Saint Maartens Dr., 1-800-952-8387, ext. 6925)

West Plains 65775, (1438 BB Hwy, 417-257-2454)

Regional Office:
St. Louis 63103 (400 South 18th St., statewide, 1-800-827-1000)

Benefits Office:
Kansas City 64128 (4801 Linwood Blvd., 816-922-2660 or 1-800-525-1483, ext. 2660)

Vet Centers:
Kansas City 64111 (3931 Main St., 816-753-1866)

St. Louis 63103 (2345 Pine St., 314-231-1260)

National Cemeteries:
Jefferson City 65101 (1024 E. McCarty St., for information, call 314-260-8720)

Springfield 65804 (1702 E. Seminole St., 417-881-9499)

St. Louis 63125 (Jefferson Barracks, 2900 Sheridan Rd., 314-260-8720)

MONTANA
Medical Centers:
Montana HC System

Fort Harrison 59636 (William St. off Hwy 12 West, 406-442-6410)

*Miles City 59301 (210 S. Winchester, 406-232-3060)

Clinics:
Anaconda, 59711 (118 E. 7th St., 406-563-6090)

Billings 59102 (2345 King Ave. W., 406-651-5670)

Bozeman 59715 (300 N. Willson, Suite #2004, 406-522-8923)

Glasgow 59230 (621 3rd St. South, 406-228-3554)

Great Falls 59405 (1417-9th St. South, Suite 200, 406-761-0179)

Miles City 59301 (210 S. Winchester, 406-232-3060

Missoula 59801 (900 North Orange, Suite 206, 406-327-0912)

Sidney 59270 (14th Ave. SW, 406-488-2307)

Kalispell 59901 (66 Claremont St., 406-751-5980)

Regional Office:
Fort Harrison 59636 (William St. off Hwy 12 West, 1-800-827-1000)

Vet Centers:
Billings 59102 (1234 Ave. C, 406-657-6071)

Missoula 59802 (500 N. Higgins Ave., 406-721-4918)

NEBRASKA

Medical Centers:
VA Nebraska-Western Iowa HC System:
*Grand Island 68803 (2201 N. Broadwell Ave., 308-382-3660 or 888-246-8745)
Lincoln 68510 (600 S. 70th St., 402-489-3802)
Omaha 68105 (4101 Woolworth Ave, 402-346-8800)

Clinics:
Alliance 69301 (524 Box Butte Ave., (308-762-8814 or 1-800-764-5370)
Gering (Scottsbluff) 69341 (2540 N. 10th St., 308-220-3930 or 1-800-764-5370)
Norfolk 68701 (2600 Norfolk Ave., Suite B, 402-346-8800)
North Platte 69101 (220 W. Leota St., 308-532-6906 or 888-246-8745)
Rushville 69360 (307 Conrad St., 308-327-2302 or 1-800-764-5370)
Sidney 69162 (645 Osage St., 308-254-5544)

Regional Office:
Lincoln 68516 (5631 S. 48th St., statewide, 1-800-827-1000)

Vet Centers:
Lincoln 68508 (920 L St., 402-476-9736)
Omaha 68131 (2428 Cuming St., 402-346-6735)

National Cemetery:
Maxwell 69151 (Fort McPherson, 12004 S. Spur 56A, 308-582-4433)

NEVADA

Medical Centers:
Ely 89301 (6 Steptoe Circle, 775-289-2788, ext. 105)
Las Vegas 89106 (1700 Vegas Dr., 702-636-3000)
*Reno 89502 (1000 Locust St., 1-888-838-6256)

Clinics:
Carson Valley 89423 (925 Ironwood St., Suite 2102, 1-888-838-6256, ext. 4000)
Henderson 89014 (2920 N. Green Valley Parkway, Suite 215, 702-456-3825)
Las Vegas 89101 (1581 N. Main St., 702-386-3140)
Pahrump 89048 (1501 E. Calvada Blvd., 775-727-6060)

Regional Office:
Reno 89520 (1201 Terminal Way, statewide, 1-800-827-1000)

Benefits Office:
Las Vegas 89106 (1500 Vegas Dr., 1-800-827-1000)

Vet Centers:
Las Vegas 89106 (1500 Vegas Dr., 702-388-6369)
Reno 89503 (1155 W. 4th St., Suite 101, 775-323-1294)

NEW HAMPSHIRE

Medical Center:
*Manchester 03104 (718 Smyth Rd., 603-624-4366 or 1-800-892-8384)

Clinics:
Littleton 03561 (600 St. Johnsbury Rd., 603-444-9328
Portsmouth 03803 (302 Newmarket St., Bldg. 15, 603-624-4366 or 1-800-892-8384)
Tilton 03276 (139 Winter St., 603-624-4366 or 1-800-892-8384)
Wolfboro 03894 (183 North Main St., 603-569-1441)
Conway 03818 (7 Greenwood Ave., 603-447-2555)

Regional Office:
Manchester 03101 (Norris Cotton Federal Bldg., 275 Chestnut St.; statewide, 1-800-827-1000)

Vet Center:
Manchester 03104 (103 Liberty St., 603-668-7060/61)

NEW JERSEY
Medical Centers:
New Jersey HC System:
  *East Orange 07018 (385 Tremont
  Ave., 973-676-1000)
  #*Lyons 07939 (151Knollkroft Rd.,
  908-647-0180)
Clinics:
Brick 08724 (970 Rt. 70, 732-206-
  8900)
Cape May 08204 (1 Monroe Ave.,
  609-898-8700)
Elizabeth 07201 (654 East Jersey
  St., 908-994-0120)
Ft. Dix 08640 (Marshall Hall, 8th &
  Alabama, 609-562-2999)
Hackensack 07601 (385 Prospect
  Ave., 201-487-1390)
Jersey City 07302 (115 Christopher
  Columbus Dr., 201-435-3055)
Morris Plains 07950 (540 West
  Hanover Ave., 973-539-9794)
Newark 07102 (20 Washington
  Place, 973-645-1441)
New Brunswick 08901 (317 George
  St., 732-729-9555)
Trenton 08611 (171 Jersey St.,
  Bldg. 36, 609-989-2355)
Turnersville 08096 (160 Fries Mill
  Rd., 856-262-4140)
Ventnor 08406 (6601 Ventnor Ave.,
  Suite 406, 609-823-3122)
Vineland 08360 (NJ Veterans
  Memorial Home, Northwest Blvd.,
  856-823-3122)
Regional Office:
Newark 07102 (20 Washington Pl.,
  statewide, 1-800-827-1000)
Vet Centers:
Jersey City 07302 (115 Christopher
  Columbus Dr., Rm., 200, 973-645-
  2038)
Newark 07102 (157 Washington St.,
  973-645-5954)
Trenton 08611 (171 Jersey St.,
  Bldg. 36, 609-989-2260)
Ventnor 08406 (6601 Ventnor Ave.,
  Suite 401, 609-487-8387)

National Cemeteries:
Beverly 08010 (916 Bridgeboro Rd.,
  609-877-5460)
Salem 08079 (Finn's Point, Fort Mott
  Rd., for information, call 609-877-
  5460)

NEW MEXICO
Medical Center:
*Albuquerque 87108 (1501 San
  Pedro Dr., SE., 505-265-1711)
Clinics:
Alamogordo 88310 (1410 Aspen,
  505-437-7000)
Artesia 88210 (1700 W. Main St.,
  505-746-3531)
Clovis 88101 (100 E. Manana St.,
  Suite 1, 505-763-4335)
Espanola 87532 (620 Coronado St,
  Suite-B, 505-753-7395)
Farmington 87401 (1001C West
  Broadway, 505-326-4383)
Gallup 87301 (1806 E. 66th Ave.,
  #5, 505-722-7234)
Hobbs 88240 (1601 N. Turner, 505-
  391-0354)
Las Cruces 88011 (1635 Don Roser,
  505-522-1241)
Raton 87740 (1275 S. 2nd St., 505-
  445-2391)
Santa Fe 87507 (465 St. Michael's
  Dr., Suite 204, 505-954-8740)
Silver City 88061 (1302 32nd St.,
  505-538-2921)
Truth or Consequences 87901 (1960
  N. Date SE, 505-894-7662)
Regional Office:
Albuquerque 87102 (Dennis Chavez
  Federal Bldg., 500 Gold Ave.,
  S.W.; statewide, 1-800-827-1000)
Vet Centers:
Albuquerque 87104 (1600 Mountain
  Rd. N.W., 505-346-6562)
Farmington 87402 (4251 E. Main,
  Suite B, 505-327-9684)
Santa Fe 87505 (2209 Brothers Rd.,
  Suite 110, 505-988-6562)

National Cemeteries:

Fort Bayard 88036 (for information, call Fort Bliss, TX, 915-564-0201)

Santa Fe 87501 (501 N. Guadalupe St., 505-988-6400, or toll-free 877-353-6295)

NEW YORK

Medical Centers:

*Albany 12208 (113 Holland Ave., 518-626-5000)

#*Bath 14810 (76 Veterans Ave., 607-664-4000)

*Bronx 10468 (130 W. Kingsbridge Rd., 718-584-9000)

NY Harbor Healthcare System:
#*Brooklyn 11209 (800 Poly Place, 718-836-6600)
#*Canandaigua 14424 (400 Fort Hill Ave., 585-394-2000)
New York 10010 (423 East 23rd St. (1st Ave.), 212-686-7500)
St. Albans 11425 (179 St. & Linden Blvd., 718-526-1000)

Hudson Valley HC System:
*Castle Point 12511 (Rte. 9D, 914-831-2000)
#*Montrose 10548 (138 Albany Post Rd., 914-737-4400)
*Northport 11768 (79 Middleville Rd., 631-261-4400)
*Syracuse 13210 (800 Irving Ave., 315-476-7461)

Western New York HC System:
*Batavia 14020 (222 Richmond Ave., 585-343-7500)
*Buffalo 14215 (3495 Bailey Ave., 716-834-9200)

Clinics:

Alexandria Bay 13607 (21 Fuller St., 315-482-4466)

Bennington 05201 (325 North St., 802-477-6913)

Binghamton 13001 (425 Robinson St., 607-772-9100)

Brooklyn 11201 (40th Flatbush Ave. Ext., 8th Floor, 718-439-4300)

Bronx 10459 (953 Southern Blvd, 718-741-4900)

Brooklyn 11208 (1205 Sutter Ave., 718-647-2600)

Brooklyn 11216 (1413 Fulton St., 718-636-4500)

Buffalo 14209 (1298 Main St., 716-551-3800)

Buffalo 14214 (2963 Main St., 716-834-881-5855)

Carmel 10512 (65 Gleneida Ave., 845-228-5292)

Catskill 12414 (159 Jefferson Hgts., Green Med. Arts Bldg., 518-943-7515)

Clifton Park 12065 (1673 Route 9, 518-383-8506)

Dunkirk 14048 (325 Central Ave., 716-366-2122)

Elizabethtown 12932 (Community Hospital, Park St., 518-873-2179)

Elmira 14901 (200 Madison Ave. 877-845-3247)

Far Rockaway 11692 (1288 Central Ave., 718-868-8230)

Fonda 12068 (2623 State Hwy 30A, 518-853-1247)

Glens Falls 12801 (84 Broad St., 518-798-6066)

Islip 11751 (39 Nassau Ave., 631-581-5330)

Jamestown 14701 (896 East 2nd St., 716-661-1447)

Kingston 12401 (63 Hurley Ave., 845-331-8322)

Lackawanna 14218 (227 Ridge Rd., 716-822-5944)

Lindenhurst 11757 (560 N. Delaware Ave., 631-261-4400, ext. 2218)

Lockport 14304 (5875 S. Transit Rd., 716-433-2025)

Lynbrook 11563 (235 Merrick Rd., 631-261-4400, ext. 2218)

Malone 12953 (115 Park St., 518-481-2545)

Massena 13662 (1 Hospital Dr., 315-764-1711)

Middletown 10949 (110 Crystal Run Rd., 845-692-0551)

Mt. Sinai 11766 (Mt. Sinai Community Ctr., N. Country Rd., 631-261-4400, ext. 2218)

Monticello 12701 (275 Broadway, 845-791-4936)

New City 10956 (Citi Bank Bldg., Suite 400, 20 Squadron Blvd. 845-634-8942)

New York 10027 (Harlem Center, 55 West 125th St., 11th Floor, 212-828-5265)

New York 10014 (Soho Center, 245 West Houston St., 212-337-2569)

Niagara Falls 14304 (620 10th St., suite 709, 716-285-8479)

Olean 14760, (500 Main St., 716-375-7555)

Oswego 13126 (County Route 45A, 315-343-0925)

Patchogue 11772 (269 Baker St. and S. Ocean Ave., 631-261-4400, ext. 2218)

Patchogue 11772 (4 Phyllis Dr. 631-758-4419)

Plainview 11803 (1425 Old Country Rd., 516-694-6008)

Plattsburgh 12901 (206 Cornelia St., Medical Bldg. Suite 307, 518-566-8563)

Port Jervis 12771 (150 Pike St. 845-856-5396)

Poughkeepsie 12603 (Freedom Exec. Park, 488 Freedom Plains Rd., Suite 120, 845-452-5151)

Riverhead 11901 (89 Hubbard Ave., 631-261-4400, ext. 2218)

Rochester 14620 (465 Westfall Rd., 716-242-0160)

Rome 13441 (125 Brookley Rd., Bldg. 510, 315-366-3389)

Sayville 11782 (400 Lakeland Ave., 631-261-4400, ext. 2218)

Schenectady 12309 (1475 Balltown Rd., 518-346-3334)

Sidney 13838 (39 Pearl St. West, 607-561-2003)

Staten Island 10304 (21 Water St., 718-815-2500)

Sunnyside 11104 (41-03 Queens Blvd., 718-741-4800)

Troy 12180 (500 Federal St., 518-274-7707)

Warsaw 14569 (400 N. Main St., 585-344-3355)

Watertown 13601 (1575 Washington St., 315-779-5050)

Wellsville 14895 (15 Loder St., 585-593-1564)

Westhampton 11978 (150 Old Riverhead Rd., 631-261-4400, ext. 5421)

White Plains 20601 (23 South Broadway, 914-421-1951)

Yonkers 10705 (118 New Main St., 914-375-8055)

Regional Offices:

Buffalo 14202 (Federal Bldg., 111 W. Huron St.; statewide, 1-800-827-1000)
(Serves counties not served by New York City Regional Office.)

New York City 10014 (245 W. Houston St.; statewide, 1-800-827-1000)
(Serves counties of Albany, Bronx, Clinton, Columbia, Delaware, Dutchess, Essex, Franklin, Fulton, Greene, Hamilton, Kings, Montgomery, Nassau, New York, Orange, Otsego, Putnam, Queens, Rensselaer, Richmond, Rockland, Saratoga, Schenectady, Schoharie, Suffolk, Sullivan, Ulster, Warren, Washington, Westchester.)

Benefits Offices:

Rochester 14620 (465 Westfall Rd., 1-800-827-1000)

Syracuse 13202 (344 W. Genesee St., 1-800-827-1000)

Vet Centers:

Albany 12206 (875 Central Ave., 518-626-6722)

Babylon 11702 (116 West Main St., 631-661-3930)

Bronx 10458 (226 E. Fordham Rd., Room 220, 718-367-3500)
Brooklyn 11201 (25 Chapel St., Suite 604, 718-330-2825)
Buffalo 14202 (564 Franklin St., 716-882-0505)
Harlem 10036 (120 W. 44th St., 212-426-2200)
New York 10027 (55 West 125th St., 212-828-5265 or 212-426-2200)
Rochester 14604 (205 St. Paul St., 585-232-5040)
Staten Island 10301 (150 Richmond Terrace, 718-816-4799)
Syracuse 13210 (716 E. Washington St., 315-478-7127)
White Plains 10601 (300 Hamilton Ave., 914-682-6251)
Woodhaven 11421 (75-10B 91st Ave., 718-296-2871)

National Cemeteries:
Bath 14810 (for information, call VA Medical Center, 607-664-4853)
Brooklyn 11208 (Cypress Hills, 625 Jamaica Ave., for information, call 631-454-4949)
Calverton 11933-1031 (210 Princeton Blvd., 631-727-5410 or 727-5770)
Elmira 14901 (Woodlawn, 1825 Davis St., for information, call 607-664-4853)
Farmingdale 11735-1211 (Long Island, 2040 Wellwood Ave., 631-454-4949)
Schuylerville 12871-1721 (Saratoga, 200 Duell Rd., 518-581-9128)

NORTH CAROLINA
Medical Centers:
*Asheville 28805 (1100 Tunnel Rd., 828-298-7911)
*Durham 27705 (508 Fulton St., 919-286-0411)
*Fayetteville 28301 (2300 Ramsey St., 910-488-2120)
*Salisbury 28144 (1601 Brenner Ave., 704-638-9000)

Clinics:
Charlotte 28262 (Presbyterian Medical Plaza, 8401 Medical Ctr. Dr., Suite 350, 704-547-0020)
Greenville 27858 (800 Moye Blvd., 252-830-2149)
Jacksonville 28546 (121 Memorial Dr., 910-577-2326)
Wilmington 28401 (1601 Physicians Dr., Suite 104, 910-362-8811)
Winston-Salem 27103 (190 Kimel Park Dr., 336-768-3296, ext. 1209 or ext. 1210)

Regional Office:
Winston-Salem 27155 (Federal Bldg., 251 N. Main St., statewide, 1-800-827-1000)

Vet Centers:
Charlotte 28202 (223 S. Brevard St., Suite 103, 704-333-6107)
Fayetteville 28311 (4140 Ramsey St., Suite 110, 910-488-6252)
Greensboro 27406 (2009 S. Elm-Eugene St., 336-333-5366)
Greenville 27858 (150 Arlington Blvd., Suite B, 252-355-7920)
Raleigh 27604 (1649 Old Louisburg Rd., 919-856-4616)

National Cemeteries:
New Bern 28560 (1711 National Ave., 252-637-2912)
Raleigh 27610-3335 (501 Rock Quarry Rd., for information, call 704-636-2661 or 636-4621)
Salisbury 28144 (202 Government Rd., 704-636-2661 or 636-4621)
Wilmington 28403 (2011 Market St., for information, call 252-637-2912)

NORTH DAKOTA
Medical Center:
*Fargo 58102 (2101 N. Elm St., 701-232-3241)

Clinics:
Bismarck 58503 (115 West Century Ave., 701-255-2252)
Grafton 58237 (West 6th St., 701-352-4594)

Minot 58705 (10 Missile Ave., 701-727-9800)

Regional Office:
Fargo 58102 (2101 Elm St., statewide, 1-800-827-1000)

Vet Centers:
Bismarck 58501 (1684 Capital Way, 701-224-9751)
Fargo 58103 (3310 Fiechtner Dr., Suite 100, 701-237-0942)
Minot 58701 (2041 3rd St. N.W., 701-852-0177)

OHIO
Medical Centers:
#*Brecksville 44141 (10000 Brecksville Rd., 440-526-3030)
*Chillicothe 45601 (17273 State Route 104, 740-773-1141)
#*Cincinnati 45220 (3200 Vine St., 513-861-3100)
Cleveland 44106 (10701 East Blvd., 216-791-3800)
#*Dayton 45428 (4100 W. 3rd St., 937-268-6511)

Clinics:
Akron 44311 (676 S. Broadway St., Suite 203, 330-344-4177)
Ashtabula 44004 (4314 Main Ave., 440-993-1318)
Athens 45701 (510 W. Union St., 740-593-7314)
Canton 44702 (221 Third St., S.E., 330-489-4600)
Cleveland/McCafferty 44113 (4242 Lorain Ave., 216-939-0699)
Columbus 43203 (542 Taylor Ave., 614-257-5200)
Eastgate 45245 (Eastgate Prof. Off. Park, 4355 Ferguson Dr., Suite 270, 513-943-3680)
E. Liverpool 43920 (332 W. 6th St., 330-386-4303)
Grove City 43123 (1955 Ohio Ave., 614-257-5800)
Lancaster 43130 (Colonnade Med. Bldg, 1550 Sheridan Dr., 740-653-6145)

Lima 45804 (1220 E. Elm St., 419-227-9676)
Lorain 44052 (205 W. 20th St., 440-244-3833)
Mansfield 44906 (1456 Park Ave. West, 419-529-4602)
Marietta 45750 (418 Colegate Dr., 740-568-0412)
Middletown 45042 (675 N. University Blvd., 513-423-8387)
Painesville 44077 (W. 7 Jackson St., 440-357-6740)
Portsmouth 45662 (621 Broadway St., 740-353-3236)
St. Clairsville 43950 (107 Plaza Dr., Suite 0, 740-695-9321)
Sandusky 44870 (3416 Columbus Ave., 419-625-7350)
Springfield 45505 (512 S. Burnett Rd., 937-328-3385)
Toledo 43614 (3333 Glendale Ave., 419-259-2000)
Warren 44485 (Riverside Sq. 1400 Tod Ave. NW, 330-392-0311)
Youngstown 44505 (2031 Belmont Ave., 330-740-9200)
Zanesville 43701 (840 Bethesda Dr., 740-453-7725)

Regional Office:
Cleveland 44199 (Anthony J. Celebrezze Fed. Bldg., 1240 E. 9th St.; statewide, 1-800-827-1000)

Benefits Offices:
Cincinnati 45202 (36 E. Seventh St., Suite 210, 1-800-827-1000)
Columbus 43215 (Federal Bldg., Rm. 309, 200 N. High St., 1-800-827-1000)

Vet Centers:
Cincinnati 45203 (801-B W. 8th St., 513-763-3500)
Cleveland Heights 44118 (2022 Lee Rd., 216-932-8471)
Columbus 43215 (30 Spruce St., 614-257-5550)
Dayton 45402 (111 W 1st St., Suite 101, 937-461-9150)

Parma 44129 (5700 Pearl Rd., Suite 102, 440-845-5023

National Cemeteries:
Dayton 45428-1008 (VA Med. Ctr., 4100 W. Third St., 937-262-2115)
Rittman 44270 (Ohio Western Reserve, 10175 Rawiga Rd., 330-335-3069)

OKLAHOMA
Medical Centers:
Muskogee 74401 (1011 Honor Heights Dr., 918-683-3261)
*Oklahoma City 73104 (921 N.E. 13th St., 405-270-0501)
Clinics:
Ardmore 73401 (1015 S. Commerce, 580-223-2266)
Lawton/Ft. Sill 73503 (Bldg. 4303, 4303 Pittman and Thomas, 580-353-1131)
McAlester 74502 (1401 E. Van Buren Ave., 918-421-8440)
Ponca City 74602 (306 Fairview, 580-765-2144)
Seminole Co. 74849 (Konawa, 527 W. Third St., 580-925-3286)
Tulsa 74145 (9322 E. 41st St., 918-764-7243)
Regional Office:
Muskogee 74401 (Federal Bldg., 125 S. Main St., 1-800-827-1000)
Benefits Office:
Oklahoma City 73102 (215 Dean A. McGee Ave., Room 276, 1-800-827-1000)
Vet Centers:
Oklahoma City 73105 (3033 N. Walnut, Suite 101W, 405-270-5184)
Tulsa 74112 (1408 S. Harvard, 918-748-5105)
National Cemeteries:
Fort Gibson 74434 (1423 Cemetery Rd., 918-478-2334)
Elgin 73538 (Fort Sill, 24665 N-S Rd. 260, 580-353-1131, Ext. 4010)

OREGON
Medical Centers:
#*Portland 97201 (3710 S.W. U.S. Veterans Hospital Rd., 503-220-8262)
*Roseburg 97470 (913 N.W. Garden Valley Blvd., 541-440-1000)
Clinics:
Bend 97701 (2115 Wyatt Court, Suite 201, 503-220-8262, ext. 55300)
Bandon 97411 (1010 1st St. S.E., Suite 100, 541-347-4736)
Brookings 97415 (412 Alder St., 541-412-1152)
Eugene 97404 (100 River Ave., 541-607-0897)
Klamath Falls 97601 (2819 Dahlia St, 541-273-6206/6129)
Salem 97301 (1660 Oak St., SE, 503-220-8262, ext. 55300)
Warrenton 97146 (Camp Rilea, 91400 Rilea Neocoxie Rd., Bldg. 7315, 503-220-8262, ext. 55300)
Domiciliary:
White City 97503 (8495 Crater Lake Hwy, 541-826-2111, ext. 3210 or 3239, 1-800-809-8725)
Regional Office:
Portland 97204 (Federal Bldg., 1220 S.W. 3rd Ave.; statewide, 1-800-827-1000)
Vet Centers:
Eugene 97403 (1255 Pearl St., 541-465-6918)
Grants Pass 97526 (211 S.E. 10th St., 541-479-6912)
Portland 97220 (8383 N.E. Sandy Blvd., Suite 110, 503-273-5370)
Salem 97301 (617 Chemeketa St., N.E., 503-362-9911)
National Cemeteries:
Eagle Point 97524 (2763 Riley Rd., 541-826-2511)
Portland 97266 (Willamette, 11800 S.E. Mt. Scott Blvd., 503-273-5250)

Roseburg 97470 (913 Garden Valley Blvd, for information, call 541-826-2511)

PENNSYLVANIA
Medical Centers:
*Altoona 16602 (2907 Pleasant Valley Blvd., 814-943-8164, toll free 877-626-2500)
#*Butler 16001 (325 New Castle Rd., 724-287-4781)
#*Coatesville 19320 (1400 Black Horse Hill Rd., 610-384-7711)
*Erie 16504 (135 E. 38th St., 814-868-8661)
*Lebanon 17042 (1700 S. Lincoln Ave., 717-272-6621, toll free 1-800-409-8771)
*Philadelphia 19104 (University & Woodland Aves., 215-823-5800, toll-free 1-800-949-1001)
Pittsburgh HC System:
Pittsburgh 15240 (University Dr. C, 412-688-6000, toll-free 1-800-309-8398)
#Pittsburgh 15206 (7180 Highland Dr., 412-363-4900, toll-free 1-800-647-6220)
*Wilkes-Barre 18711 (1111 East End Blvd.,1-877-928-2621, toll-free)
Clinics:
Aliquippa 15001 (2304 Broadhead Rd., 724-378-6640)
Allentown 18103 (3110 Hamilton Blvd., 610-776-4304, toll-free 1-866-249-6472)
Berwick 18603 (301 West 3rd St., 570-759-0351)
Brookville 15825 (298 Main St., 724-285-2577, toll free 1-800-362-8262, ext. 2577)
Camp Hill 17011 (25 N. 32nd St., 717-730-9782)
DuBois 15801 (90 Beaver Dr., Rice Complex, Bldg. D, Suite 213, 814-375-6817)
Frackville 17931 (10 East Spruce St., 570-874-4289)

Greensburg 15601 (1275 S. Main St., Suite 203, 724-830-8762)
Johnstown 15904 (108 College Park Plaza, 814-266-8696)
Kittanning 16201 (1 Nolte Dr., 724-285-2577, toll-free 1-800-362-8262 ext. 2577)
Knox 16232 (400 Huston Ave., 724-285-2577, toll-free 1-800-362-8262 ext. 2577)
Lancaster 17601 (Greenfield Corporate Center, 1861 Charter Lane, Suite 118, 717-290-6900)
Levittown 19055 (7321 New Falls Rd, 215-547-3423)
Meadville 16335 (18955 Park Ave. Plaza, 814-337-0170)
Pottsville 17901 (Schuykill Co., GSH Reg. Med. Ctr., 700 E. Norwegian St., 570-621-4115)
Reading 19601 (145 N. Sixth St., 3rd floor, St. Jos. Med. Ctr., Community Campus, 610-208-4717)
Sayre 18840 (301 N. Elmira, 570-888-6803, toll-free 1-877-470-0920)
State College 16801 (3048 Enterprise Dr., Ferguson Square, 814-867-5415)
Schuylkill Haven 17972 (Orwigsburg (South), 6 S. Greenview Rd., 570-366-3915)
Smethport 16749 (406 Franklin St, 814-887-5655)
Spring City 19475 (11 Independence Dr., 610-948-0981)
Springfield 19064 (489 Baltimore Pike, 610-543-1588)
Tobyhanna 18466 (Bldg. 220, Tobyhanna Army Depot, 570-895-8341)
Washington County 15301 (997 N. Main St., 724-250-7790)
Williamsport 17701 (805 Penn St., 570-322-4791)
Willow Grove 19090 (1120 Fairchild St., Bldg. 236, 215-773-2620)

York 17403 (1796 3rd Ave., 717-854-2481)

Regional Offices:

Philadelphia 19101 (RO and Insurance Center, P.O. Box 8079, 5000 Wissahickon Ave., RO, 1-800-827-1000; insurance, local, 842-2000, nationwide1-800-669-8477; Serves counties of Adams, Berks, Bradford, Bucks, Cameron, Carbon, Centre, Chester, Clinton, Columbia, Cumberland, Dauphin, Delaware, Franklin, Juniata, Lackawanna, Lancaster, Lebanon, Lehigh, Luzerne, Lycoming, Mifflin, Monroe, Montgomery, Montour, Northampton, Northumberland, Perry, Philadelphia, Pike, Potter, Schuylkill, Snyder, Sullivan, Susquehanna, Tioga, Union, Wayne, Wyoming, York)

Pittsburgh 15222 (1000 Liberty Ave.; statewide, 1-800-827-1000, Serves the remaining counties of Pennsylvania.)

Benefits Office:

Wilkes-Barre 18702 (Jewelcor Bldg., 2nd Floor, 100 N. Wilkes-Barre Blvd., 1-800-827-1000)

Vet Centers:

Erie 16501 (1001 State St., Suites 1&2, 814-453-7955)

Harrisburg 17102 (1500 N. 2nd St., Suite 2, 717-782-3954)

McKeesport 15131 (2001 Lincoln Way, 412-678-7704)

Philadelphia 19107 (801 Arch St., Suite 102, 215-627-0238)

Philadelphia 19152 (101 E. Olney Ave., 215-924-4670)

Pittsburgh 15222 (954 Penn Ave., 412-765-1193)

Scranton 18505 (1002 Pittston Ave., 570-344-2676)

Williamsport 17701 (805 Penn St., 570-327-5281)

National Cemeteries:

Annville 17003-9618 (Indiantown Gap, R.R. 2, P.O. Box 484, 717-865-5254)

Philadelphia 19138 (Haines St. & Limekiln Pike, for information, call 609-877-5460)

PHILIPPINES

Regional Office:

Manila 0930 (1131 Roxas Blvd., 011-632-523-1001, International Mailing Address: PSC 501, FPO AP 96515-1100)

Clinic:

Manila 1300 (2201 Roxas Blvd., Pasay City, 011-632-833-4566)

PUERTO RICO

Medical Center:

*San Juan 00921-3201 (10 Casia St., 787-641-7582)

Clinics:

Arecibo 00612 (Galle Gonzalo Marín #50, 787-816-1818)

Mayaguez 00680 (Ave. Hostos 345, 787-834-6900 or 1-800-569-2356)

Ponce 00716-2001 (#10 Paseo del Veterano, 787-812-3030)

St. Croix 00850-4701 (The Village Mall, Plot #113, Kingshill, 340-778-5553)

St. Thomas 00802 (Bucaneer Mall, Suite #103-104, 340-774-6674)

Regional Office:

San Juan 00918 (150 Carlos Chardon Ave., Hato Rey; For mail: P.O. Box 364867, San Juan, PR 00936. All Puerto Rico and the Virgin Islands, 1-800-827-1000)

Benefits Offices:

Mayaguez 00680 (Ave. Hostos 345, Carretera 2, Frente al Centro Medico, 1-800-827-1000)

Ponce 00731 (Reparada Industrial , Lot # 1 Calle Principal, 1-800-827-1000)

Vet Centers:

Arecibo 00612-4702 (52 Gonzalo Marin St., 787-879-4510 or 879-4581)

Ponce 00731 (35 Mayol St., 787-841-3260)

San Juan 00921 (Condominio Med. Ctr. Plaza, Suite LC8A and LC9, La Riviera, 787-749-4409)

National Cemetery:

Bayamon 00960 (Ave. Cementerio Nacional #50, Barrio Hato Tejas, 787-798-7620)

RHODE ISLAND
Medical Center:

Providence 02908 (830 Chalkstone Ave., 401-273-7100)

Clinic:

Middletown 02842 (One Corporate Pl., West Main Rd., 401-457-8057)

Regional Office:

Providence 02903 (380 Westminster St.; statewide, 1-800-827-1000)

Vet Center:

Warwick 02889 (2038 Warwick Ave., 401-739-0167)

SOUTH CAROLINA
Medical Centers:

Charleston 29401 (109 Bee St., 843-577-5011)

*Columbia 29209-1639 (6439 Garners Ferry Rd., 803-776-4000)

Clinics:

Beaufort 29902 (1 Pinckney Blvd., 843-770-0444)

Florence 29501 (514H Dargan St., 843-292-8383)

Greenville 29605 (3510 Augusta Rd., 864-299-1600)

Myrtle Beach 29577 (3381 Phillis Blvd., 843-477-0177)

Rock Hill 29732 (124 Glenwood Dr., 803-328-3622)

Sumter 29150 (407 N. Salem St., 803-938-9901)

Orangeburg 29118 (1767 Villagepark Dr., 803-533-1335)

Regional Office:

Columbia 29201 (1801 Assembly St.; statewide, 1-800-827-1000)

Vet Centers:

Columbia 29201 (1513 Pickens St., 803-765-9944)

Greenville 29601 (14 Lavinia Ave., 864-271-2711)

North Charleston 29406 (5603A Rivers Ave., 843-747-8387)

National Cemeteries:

Beaufort 29902-3947 (1601 Boundary St., 843-524-3925)

Florence 29501 (803 E. National Cemetery Rd., 843-669-8783)

SOUTH DAKOTA
Medical Centers:

Black Hills HC System:
   *Fort Meade 57741 (113 Comanche Rd., 605-347-2511 or 1-800-743-1070)
   #Hot Springs 57747 (500 N. 5th St., 605-745-2000 or 1-800-764-5370)

*Sioux Falls 57105 (2501 W. 22nd St., 605-336-3230 or 1-800-316-8387)

Clinics:

Aberdeen 57401 (1440 15th Ave NW, 605-622-2640)

Eagle Butte 57625 (15 Main St., 605-964-8000 or 1-800-764-5370)

Pierre 57501 (1601 N. Harrison, Suite 1A , 605-945-1710 or 1-800-743-1070)

Rapid City 57701 (3625 5th St., 605-718-1095 or 1-800-743-1070)

Rosebud 57570 (Soldier Creek Rd., Hwy 18, 605-747-2231 or 1-800-764-5370)

Winner 57580 (915 E. 8th St., 605-842-2243 or 1-800-764-5370)

McLauglin 57642 (Silver Barn Rd., 605-823-4574 or 1-800-743-1070)

Regional Office:

Sioux Falls 57117 (2501 W. 22nd St.; statewide, 1-800-827-1000)

Vet Centers:

Martin 57551 (East Hwy 18, 605-685-1300)

Rapid City 57701 (610 Kansas City St., 605-348-0077)

Sioux Falls 57104 (601 S. Cliff Ave., Suite C, 605-332-0856)

National Cemeteries:

Hot Springs 57747 (500 N. 5th St., 605-347-3830 or 347-7299)

Sturgis 57785 (Black Hills, I-90, Exit 34, 605-347-3830 or 347-7299)

Sturgis 57785 (Fort Meade, Old Stone Rd., for information, call 605-347-3830 or 347-7299)

TENNESSEE

Medical Centers:

*Memphis 38104 (1030 Jefferson Ave., 901-523-8990)

#*Mountain Home 37684 (Sidney & Lamont St., 423-926-1171)

VA Tennessee Valley Healthcare System:
Nashville 37212 (1310 24th Ave., South, 615-327-4751)

Clinics:

Chattanooga 37411 (East Gate Center, 150 Debra Rd., Bldg 6200, Suite 5200, 423-893-6500)

Clarksville 37042 (Gateway Med. Ctr., Suite 110, 1731 Madison St., 931-221-2172)

Cookeville 38501 (Primary Care, 1101 Neal St., 931-525-1652)

Cookeville 38502 (Mental Health Care, 1200 South Willow Ave., 931-432-4123)

Dover 37058-0497 (1201 Spring St., 931-232-5329)

Savannah 38372 (150 East End Dr., for informaction, call 901-523-8990)

Knoxville 37923 (9031 Cross Park Dr., 865-545-4592)

Mountain City 37683 (1901 S. Shady St., 423-727-5900)

Rogersville 37857 (851 Locust St., 423-272-5202)

Tullahoma 37389 (225 First St., Arnold AFB, 931-454-6134)

Regional Office:

Nashville 37203 (110 9th Ave. South; statewide, 1-800-827-1000)

Vet Centers:

Chattanooga 37411 (951 Eastgate Loop Rd., Bldg. 5700, Suite 300, 423-855-6570)

Johnson City 37604 (1615A W. Market St., 423-928-8387)

Knoxville 37914 (2817 E. Magnolia Ave., 423-545-4680)

Memphis 38104 (1835 Union, Suite 100, 901-544-0173)

National Cemeteries:

Chattanooga 37404 (1200 Bailey Ave., 423-855-6590)

Knoxville 37917 (939 Tyson St., N.W., for information, call 423-855-6590)

Madison 37115-4619 (Nashville, 1420 Gallatin Rd. So., 615-736-2839)

Memphis 38122 (3568 Townes Ave., 901-386-8311)

Mountain Home 37684 (VA Medical Center, Bldg. 117, 423-979-3535)

TEXAS

Medical Centers:

*Amarillo 79106 (6010 Amarillo Blvd. West, 806-355-9703)

*Houston 77030 (2002 Holcombe Blvd., 713-791-1414)

West Texas HC System
*Big Spring 79720 (300 Veterans Blvd., 800-472-1365)

Central Texas HC System:
*Marlin 76661 (1016 Ward St., 254-883-3511 or 1-800-423-2111)
#*Temple 76504 (1901 Veterans Memorial Dr., 800-423-2111 or commercial 254-778-4811)

Waco 76711 (4800 Memorial Dr., 254-752-6581 or 1-800-423-2111)

North Texas HC System:
#*Bonham 75418 (1201 East Ninth St., 800-924-8387)
#*Dallas 75216 (4500 S. Lancaster Rd., 800-849-3597)

South Texas HC System:
*San Antonio 78284 (7400 Merton Minter Blvd., 210-617-5657)
*Kerrville 78028 (3600 Memorial Blvd., 830-792-2020)

Clinics:
Abilene 78606 (4225 Woods Place, 915-695-3252)
Austin 78741 (2901 Montopolis Dr., 512-389-1010)
Beaumont 77707 (3420 Veteran Circle, 409-981-8550)
Beeville 78102 (302 South Hillside Dr., 888-686-6350)
Bishop 78343 (301 W. Main, 888-686-6350)
Bonham (Grayson, Delta, and Lamar Counties, 800-924-8387, ext. 36676 or commercial 903-583-6676)
Brownsville 78520 (394 Military Rd., 888-686-6350)
Brownwood 76801 (125 S. Park Dr., Suite A, 915-641-0568)
Childress 79201 (Hwy 83 North, 940-937-3636)
Cleburne (Johnson and Ellis Counties, 800-849-3597, ext. 71465 or commercial 214-857-1465)
College Station 77845 (1605 Rock Prairie Rd., Suite 212, 409-680-0361)
Corpus Christi 78405 (5283 Old Brownsville Rd., 361-854-7392, ext. 227)
Decatur (Wise, Jack, Clay, Archer, Baylor, Young, Throckmorton and Montague Counties, 800-849-3597, ext. 36342 or commercial 214-857-1465)

Denton (Denton, Cooke and Collin Counties, 800-924-8387, ext. 36676or comm. 903-583-6676)
Eagle Pass 78852 (2525 Loop 431, 888-686-6350)
Eastland (Eastland, Parker, Palo Pinto, Hood, Callahan and Stephens Counties, 800-849-3597, ext. 71465 or commercial 214-857-1465)
El Paso 79930 (5001 N. Piedras St., 915-564-6100)
Fort Stockton 79735 (Sanderson Hwy, 915-336-8365)
Fort Worth 76104 (300 W. Rosedale St., 800-443-9672)
Greenville (Kaufman, Hopkins, Hunt, Rockwall, Titus and Franklin Counties, 800-849-3597, ext. 71465 or comm. 214-857-1465)
Hamilton 76531 (400 N. Brown St., 254-386-3102)
Laredo 78043 (2359 E. Saunders Ave., 956-725-7060)
Longview 75601 (1205 E. Marshall Ave., 903-247-8262)
Lubbock 79410 (4902 34th St., Suite 10, 806-796-7900)
Lufkin 75904 (1301 W. Frank Ave., 936-633-2700)
McAllen 78503 (2101 S. Colonel Rowe Blvd., 956-618-7103)
Northeast Bexar Co. 78233 (12702 Toepperwein, Suite 102, 210-617-4020)
Northeast Bexar Co. 78217 (2455 NE Loop 410, Suite 100, 210-617-4020)
Northwest Bexar Co. 78229 (4600 NW Loop 410, Suite 110, 210-617-4020)
Northwest Bexar Co. 78238 (6218 NW Loop 410, 210-617-4020)
Odessa 79761 (419 W. Fourth St., 915-580-4560)
Palestine, 75801 (3215 W. Oak Blvd., Suite 200, 903-723-9006)

Red River Co. 75462 (call 800-924-8387, ext. 36342 or commercial 903-583-6342)

San Angelo 76905 (2018 Pulliam, 915-658-6138)

San Antonio 78240 (5788 Eckert Rd., 210-699-2133 or 2125)

San Diego 78384 (102 E. King, Suite 200, 888-686-6350)

South Bexar County 78223 (1055 Ada, San Antonio, 210-358-5701)

Southeast Bexar Co. 78222 (4243 E. Southcross, Suite 205, 210-617-4020)

Southeast Dallas Co. 75217 (call 800-849-3597, ext. 71465 or commercial 214-857-1465)

Stamford 79553 (1303 Mabee Dr., 915-773-5733)

Stratford 79084 (1220 Purnell St., 806-396-2852)

Tarrant Co. 76106 (call 800-924-8387, ext. 36676 or commercial 903-583-6676)

Texarkana 75503 (2717 Summerhill Rd., 903-793-3371)

Tyler, 75217 (Smith, Camp, Henderson, Van Zandt, Rains and Wood Counties, call 800-849-3597, ext. 71465 or commercial 214-857-1465)

Uvalde 78801 (1025 Garner Field Rd., 888-686-6350)

Victoria 77901 (4206 Retama Circle, 361-572-0006, ext. 225)

Wichita Falls 76301 (1410 Eighth St., 940-723-2373)

Regional Offices:

Houston 77030 (6900 Almeda Rd., statewide, 1-800-827-1000. Serves counties of Angelina, Aransas, Atacosa, Austin, Bandera, Bee, Bexar, Blanco, Brazoria, Brewster, Brooks, Caldwell, Calhoun, Cameron, Chambers, Colorado, Comal, Crockett, DeWitt, Dimitt, Duval, Edwards, Fort Bend, Frio, Galveston, Gillespie, Goliad, Gonzales, Grimes, Guadeloupe, Hardin, Harris, Hays, Hidalgo, Houston, Jackson, Jasper, Jefferson, Jim Hogg, Jim Wells, Karnes, Kendall, Kenedy, Kerr, Kimble, Kinney, Kleberg, LaSalle, Lavaca, Liberty, Live Oak, McCulloch, McMullen, Mason, Matagorda, Maverlck, Medina, Menard, Montgomery, Nacogdoches, Newton, Nueces, Orange, Pecos, Polk, Real, Refugio, Sabine, San Augustine, San Jacinto, San Patricio, Schleicher, Shelby, Starr, Sutton, Terrell, Trinity, Tyler, Uvalde, Val Verde, Victoria, Walker, Waller, Washington, Webb, Wharton, Willacy, Wilson, Zapata, Zavala)

Waco 76799 (One Veterans Plaza, 701 Clay; statewide, 1-800-827-1000; serves the rest of the state. In Bowie County, the City of Texarkana is served by Little Rock, AR, Regional Office, 1-800-827-1000.)

Benefits Offices:

Corpus Christi 78405 (5283 Old Brownsville Rd., 1-800-827-1000)

Dallas 75216 (4500 S. Lancaster Rd., 1-800-827-1000)

El Paso 79930 (5001 Piedras Dr., 1-800-827-1000)

Lubbock 79410 (4902 34th St., Suite 10, Rm. 134, 1-800-827-1000)

McAllen 78503 (2102 S. Colonial Rowe Blvd., 1-800-827-1000)

San Antonio 78240 (5788 Eckert Rd., 1-800-827-1000)

Tyler 75701 (1700 SSE Loop 323, Suite 310, 1-800-827-1000)

Vet Centers:

Amarillo 79109 (3414 Olsen Blvd., Suite E., 806-354-9779)

Austin 78745 (1110 W. Wm. Cannon Dr., Suite 301, 512-416-1314)

Corpus Christi 78411 (4646 Corona, Suite 110, 361-854-9961)

Dallas 75244 (5232 Forest Lane, Suite 111, 214-361-5896)

El Paso 79925 (Sky Park II, 6500 Boeing, Suite L-112, 915-772-5368)

Fort Worth 76104 (1305 W. Magnolia, Suite B, 817-921-9095)

Houston 77006 (503 Westheimer, 713-523-0884)

Houston 77024 (701 N. Post Oak Rd., Suite 102, 713-682-2288)

Laredo 78041 (6020 McPherson Rd. #1A, 956-723-4680)

Lubbock 79410 (3208 34th St., 806-792-9782)

McAllen 78504 (801 Nolana Loop, Suite 115, 956-631-2147)

Midland 79703 (3404 W. Illinois, Suite 1, 915-697-8222)

San Antonio 78210 (231 W. Cypress St., 210-472-4025)

National Cemeteries:

Dallas-Fort Worth 75211 (2000 Mountain Creek Pkwy., 214-467-3374)

Fort Bliss 79906 (5200 Fred Wilson Rd., 915-564-0201)

Houston 77038 (10410 Veterans Memorial Dr., 281-447-8686 or 447-0580)

Kerrville 78028 (3600 Memorial Blvd., for information, call 210-820-3891 or 820-3894)

San Antonio 78209 (Fort Sam Houston, 1520 Harry Wurzbach Rd., 210-820-3891 or 820-3894)

San Antonio 78202 (517 Paso Hondo St., for information, call 210-820-3891 or 820-3894)

UTAH

Medical Center:

Salt Lake City 84148 (500 Foothill Dr., 801-582-1565)

Clinics:

Fountain Green 84632 (300 W. 300 S., 435-623-3129)

Milford 84751 (451 N. Main, 435-623-3129)

Nephi 84648 (South Central Clinic, 48 W. 1500 N., 435-623-3129)

Ogden 84405 (Medical Arts Bldg., 2nd Floor, Suite 205, 5405 S. 500 East, 801-479-4105)

Orem 84057 (Timpanogos Med. Off. Bldg., 4th Floor, Suite 440, 740 W. 800 North, 801- 235-0953)

Roosevelt 84066 (210 West 300 North (75-3), 435-722-3971)

St. George 84770 (1100 E. Tabernacle, 435-634-7608)

Regional Office:

Salt Lake City 84147 (Federal Bldg., 125 S. State St., statewide, 1-800-827-1000)

Vet Centers:

Provo 84601 (750 North 200 West, Suite 105, 801-377-1117)

Salt Lake City 84106 (1354 East 3300 South, 801-584-1294)

VERMONT

Medical Center:

White River Junction 05009 (215 N. Main St., 802-295-9363)

Clinics:

Bennington 05201 (325 North St., 802-447-6913)

Colchester 05446 (74 Hegeman Ave., 802-655-1356)

Rutland 05702 (215 Stratton Rd., 802-773-3386)

Regional Office:

White River Junction 05009 (215 N. Main St., 802-296-5177, or 1-800-827-1000 from within Vermont)

Vet Centers:

South Burlington 05403 (359 Dorset St., 802-862-1806)

White River Junction 05001 (Gilman Off. Ctr., Bldg. #2, Holiday Inn Dr., 802-295-2908 or 1-800-649-6603)

VIRGINIA

Medical Centers:
#*Hampton 23667 (100 Emancipation Dr., 757-722-9961)
*Richmond 23249 (1201 Broad Rock Blvd., 804-675-5000)
*Salem 24153 (1970 Roanoke Blvd., 540-982-2463)

Clinics:
Alexandria 22309 (8796-D Sacramento Dr., 703-719-6797)
Danville 24541 (2811 Riverside Dr., 804-799-1200)
Fredericksburg 22401 (1965 Jeff. Davis Hwy, 540-370-4468)
Harrisonburg 22802 (101 North Main St., Suite 220 Harrison Plaza, 540-442-1773)
Norton 24273 (Third St. N.E., 540-679-9107)
Stephens City 22655 (106 Hyde Court, 540-869-0600)
Tazewell 24651 (123 Ben Holt Ave. 540-988-2526)

Regional Offices:
Roanoke 24011 (210 Franklin Rd., S.W. statewide, 1-800-827-1000)
Northern Virginia counties of Arlington & Fairfax, cities of Alexandria, Fairfax, Falls Church served by Washington, D.C., RO, 1-800-827-1000).

Vet Centers:
Alexandria 22309 (8796 Sacramento Dr., Suite D&E, 703-360-8633)
Norfolk 23517 (2200 Colonial Ave., Suite 3, 757-623-7584)
Richmond 23230 (4202 Fitzhugh Ave., 804-353-8958)
Roanoke 24016 (350 Albemarle Ave., SW, 540-342-9726)

National Cemeteries:
Alexandria 22314 (1450 Wilkes St., for information, call 703-690-2217; or toll-free from Wash., DC, metro area 703-221-2183)
Culpeper 22701 (305 U.S. Ave., 540-825-0027)
Danville 24541 (721 Lee St., for information, call 704-636-2661)
Hampton 23667 (Cemetery Rd. at Marshall Ave., 757-723-7104)
Hopewell 23860 (City Point, 10th Ave. & Davis St., for information, call 804-795-2031)
Leesburg 22075 (Balls Bluff, Rte. 7, for information, call 540-825-0027)
Mechanicsville 23111 (Cold Harbor, Rt. 156 North, for information, call 804-795-2031)
Richmond 23231 (Fort Harrison, 8620 Varina Rd., for information, call 804-795-2031)
Richmond 23231 (Glendale, 8301 Willis Church Rd., for information, call 804-795-2031)
Richmond 23231 (1701 Williamsburg Rd., for information, call 804-795-2031)
Sandston 23150 (Seven Pines, 400 E. Williamsburg Rd., for information, call 804-795-2031)
St. Charles 24282 (100 Main St., 540-383-4428)
Staunton 24401 (901 Richmond Ave., for information, call 540-825-0027)
Triangle 22172 (Quantico, 18424 Joplin Rd. (Rte. 619), 703-690-2217; or toll-free from Wash., DC, metro area 703-221-2183)
Winchester 22601 (401 National Ave., for information, call 540-825-0027)

VIRGIN ISLANDS
For information on VA benefits, call 1-800-827-1000.

Vet Centers:
St. Croix 00850 (Box 12, R.R. 02, Village Mall, #113, 340-778-5553)
St. Thomas 00802 (9800 Buccaneer Mall, Suite 8, 340-774-6674)

WASHINGTON
Medical Centers:
Puget Sound HC System:
*Seattle 98108 (1660 S.
Columbian Way, 206-762-1010)
#*Tacoma 98493 (9600 Veterans
Dr., S.W., American Lake, 253-
582-8440)
*Spokane 99205 (4815 N. Assembly
St., 509-434-7000)
*Walla Walla 99362 (77 Wainwright
Dr., 509-525-5200)
Clinics:
Bremerton 98310 (925 Adele Ave.,
360-782-0129)
Tri-Cities 99352 (Richland, 948
Stevens Dr., Suite C, 509-946-
1020)
Yakima 98902 (310 N 5th Ave., 509-
457-2736)
Regional Office:
Seattle 98174 (Fed. Bldg., 915 2nd
Ave., statewide, 1-800-827-1000)
Benefits Office:
Fort Lewis 98433 (Waller Hall, Rm.
700, 253-967-7106)
Vet Centers:
Bellingham 98226 (3800 Byron Ave.,
Suite 124, 360-733-9226)
Seattle 98121 (2030 9th Ave., Suite
210, 206-553-2706)
Spokane 99206 (100 N. Mullan Rd.,
Suite 102, 509-444-8387)
Tacoma 98409 (4916 Center St.,
Suite E, 253-565-7038)
Yakima 98901 (310 N. 5th Ave., 509-
457-2736)
National Cemetery:
Kent 98042-4868 (Tahoma, 18600
S.E. 240th St., 425-413-9614)

WEST VIRGINIA
Medical Center:
*Beckley 25801 (200 Veterans Ave.,
304-255-2121)
Clarksburg 26301 (1 Medical Center
Dr., 304-623-3461)
Huntington 25704 (1540 Spring
Valley Dr., 304-429-6741)

#*Martinsburg 25401 (Route 9, 304-
263-0811 or 1-800-817-3807)
Clinics:
Charleston 25304 (104 Alex Lane,
304-926-6001)
Franklin 26807 (305 North Main St.,
304-358-2355)
Gassaway 26624 (707 Elk St., 304-
364-5654)
Parkersburg 26101 (912 Market St.,
304-422-5114)
Parsons 26287 (206 Spruce St.,
304-478-2219)
Petersburg 26847 (Grant Memorial
Hospital, Route 55 West, 304-257-
1026, ext. 120)
Regional Office:
Huntington 25701 (640 Fourth Ave.,
statewide, 1-800-827-1000;
counties of Brooke, Hancock,
Marshall, Ohio, served by
Pittsburgh, Pa., Regional Office)
Vet Centers:
Beckley 25801 (101 Ellison Ave.,
304-252-8220)
Charleston 25302 (521 Central Ave.,
304-343-3825)
Huntington 25701 (1005 6th Ave.,
304-523-8387)
#Martinsburg 25401 (900 Winches-
ter Ave., 304-263-6776)
Morgantown 26508 (1083 Greenbag
Rd. 304-291-4303)
Princeton 24740 (905 Mercer St.,
304-425-5653)
Wheeling 26003 (1206 Chapline St.,
304-232-0587)
National Cemeteries:
Grafton 26354 (431 Walnut St., for
information, call 304-265-2044)
Grafton 26354 (West Virginia, Rt. 2,
Box 127, 304-265-2044)

WISCONSIN
Medical Centers:
Madison 53705 (2500 Overlook
Terrace, 608-256-1901)
#*Milwaukee 53295 (5000 W.
National Ave., 414-384-2000)

*Tomah 54660 (500 E. Veterans St., 608-372-3971)

Clinics:
Appleton 54914 (10 Tri-Park Way, 920-831-0070)
Baraboo 53913 (626 14th St., 608-280-7038)
Beaver Dam 53916 (208 LaCrosse St., 608-280-7038)
Chippewa Falls 54729 (Eau Claire, 2503 County Rd. I, 715-720-3780)
Cleveland 53015 (1205 North Ave., 920-693-3750)
Edgerton 53534 (92 E. Hwy 59, 608-280-7038)
LaCrosse 54601-3200 (2600 State Rd., 608-784-3886)
Loyal 54446 (141 North Main St., 715-255-9799)
Rhinelander 54501 (5 W. Frederick, 715-362-4080)
Superior 54880 (3520 Tower Ave., 715-392-9711)
Union Grove 53182 (21425 Spring St., 262-878-7820)
Wausau 54401 (995 Campus Dr., 715-675-3391)
Wisconsin Rapids 54494 (420 Dewey St., 715-422-7736)

Regional Office:
Milwaukee 53295 (5000 W. National Ave., Bldg. 6, statewide, 1-800-827-1000)

Vet Centers:
Madison 53703 (147 S. Butler St., 608-264-5342)
Milwaukee 53218 (5401 N. 76th St., 414-536-1301)

National Cemetery:
Milwaukee 53295-4000 (Wood, 5000 W. National Ave., Bldg. 1301, 414-382-5300)

WYOMING
Medical Centers
*Cheyenne 82001 (2360 E. Pershing Blvd., 307-778-7550)
*Sheridan 82801 (1898 Fort Rd., 307-672-3473)

Clinics:
Casper 82601 (111 South Jefferson St., Suite 105, 307-235-4143)
Gillette 82718 (1701 Phillips Circle, Suite A, 307-685-0676)
Green River 82935 (1400 Uinta Dr., 307-875-6010, ext. 257)
Powell 82435 (777 Ave. H, 307-754-7257)
Riverton 82501 (2300 Rose Lane, 307-857-1211)

Benefits Office:
Cheyenne 82001 (2360 E. Pershing Blvd., statewide, 1-800-827-1000)

Vet Centers:
Casper 82601 (111 S. Jefferson, Suite 100, 307-261-5355)
Cheyenne 82001 (2424 Pioneer Ave., Suite 103, 307-778-7370)

Bonus Section: The VA Online

The Department of Veterans Affairs (VA) Web site is a worldwide resource that provides information on VA programs, veterans benefits, VA facilities worldwide, and VA medical automation software. Made available in September 1994, the site serves several major constituencies, including the veteran and his or her dependents, Veterans Service Organizations, the military, the general public, and VA employees around the world. These documents are easily accessible and richly linked from their table of contents, as well as searchable by keyword.

Internet mail is also available, which allows veterans to make specific inquiries and receive official responses from the VA staff. In addition to providing the text of this book, press releases, and announcements of interest to veterans, a listing of current job opportunities with the VA and many of the most requested benefit application and information forms are now available to you.

The VA Web site can be accessed at www.va.gov.

Forms Online

When you access the Veterans Benefits Administration site at www.va.gov/forms, you can follow links to many online forms. Many of these forms have multiple pages. To complete a form, you need to download all its pages. These forms are in three formats: Adobe Acrobat Portable Document Format (PDF), Microsoft Word templates (DOT), and Graphical Interchange Format (GIF) If you experience difficulty reading or interpreting either the form or instructions, please call your local VA office or the VA toll free number, 1-800-827-1000. To submit the form, please contact your local VA office for instructions.

The following sections detail forms that are available online.

The Most Popular VA Benefits Forms

The most frequently downloaded VA forms are the following. To receive a printed copy of a form, call the toll-free number next to it or the General Contact TDD, 1-800-827-4833.

Compensation & Pension Program Application (21-526)
1-800-827-1000 or apply online at VONAPP.

Education Application (22-1990)
1-888-442-4551 or apply online at VONAPP.

Home Loan Guaranty - Certificate of Eligibility (26-1880)
1-888-244-6711 - Eastern US - East of the Mississippi River
1-888-487-1970 - Western US - West of the Mississippi River

Vocational Rehabilitation & Employment Application (28-1900)
1-800-827-1000 or apply online at VONAPP.

Insurance Designation of Beneficiary (29-336)
1-800-669-8477

Request Pertaining to Military Records (SF 180)
National Archives and Records Administration

106

General VBA Forms

20-572   Request For Change Of Address/Cancellation Of Direct Deposit (1 page)

20-8800   Request For VA Forms and Publications (1 page)

Compensation and Pension Forms

21-22   Appointment of Veterans Service Organization as Claimant's Representative (5 pages)**NEW**

21a -   Application For Accreditation As A Claims Agent (3 pages)

21-0304   Application for Benefits for Certain Children with Disabilities Born of Vietnam Veterans (4 pages)

21-0501   Veterans Benefits Timetable (2 pages)

21-0506   Notice of Your Due Process Rights (1 page)

21-0510   Eligibility Verification Report Instructions (4 pages)

21-0511s-1 Old Law Eligibility Verification Report (Surviving Spouse)(8 pages)

21-0512s-1 Section 306 Eligibility Verification Report (Surviving Spouse) (2 pages)

21-0513-1 Old Law and Section 306 Eligibility Verification Report (2 pages)

21-0514-1 Parent's DIC Eligibility Verification Report (2 pages)

21-0516-1 Improved Pension Eligibility Verification Report (Veteran With No Children) (2 pages)

21-0518-1 Improved Pension Eligibility Verification Report (Surviving Spouse With No Children) (2 pages)

21-0519c-1 Improved Pension Eligibility Verification Report (Child or Children) (2 pages)

21-526   Veteran's Application for Compensation or Pension (24 pages). Apply online at VONAPP.

21-527   Income-Net Worth And Employment Statement (6 pages)

21-530   Application For Burial Benefits (Under 38 U.S.C. Chapter 23) (4 pages)

21-534   Application for Dependency and Indemnity Compensation, Death Pension and Accrued Benefits by a Surviving Spouse or Child (Including Death Compensation if Applicable) (12 pages)

21-535   Application for Dependency and Indemnity Compensation by Parent(s) (10 pages)

21-601   Application For Reimbursement From Accrued Amounts Due A Deceased Beneficiary (2 pages)

21-674   Request For Approval of School Attendance (4 pages)

21-686c   Declaration of Status of Dependents (2 pages)

21-2008   Application For United States Flag For Burial Purposes (3 pages)

21-2680   Examination For Housebound Status or Permanent Need For Regular Aid and Attendance (2 pages)

21-4138   Statement in Support of Claim (1 page)

21-4142	Authorization And Consent To Release Information To The Department of Veterans Affairs (VA) (2 pages)
21-4169	Supplement to VA Forms 21-526, 21-534, and 21-535 (4 pages)
21-4176	Report of Accidental Injury in Support of Claim for Compensation or Pension (2 pages)
21-4192	Request For Employment Information in Connection With Claim For Disability Benefits (1 page)
21-4502	Application For Automobile Or Other Conveyance and Adaptive Equipment (Under 38 U.S.C. 3901-3904) (5 pages)
21-4706b	Federal Fiduciary's Account (2 pages)
21-4718a	Certificate of Balance On Deposit and Authorization to Disclose Financial Records (2 pages)
21-6753	Original Or Amended Dependency and Indemnity Compensation Award (2 pages)
21-8049	Request for Details of Expenses (2 pages)
21-8416	Medical Expense Report (2 pages)
21-8678	Application For Annual Clothing Allowance (1 page)
21-8764	Disability Compensation Award Attachment Important Information (2 pages)
21-8940	Veteran's Application For Increased Compensation Based On Unemployability (2 pages)
21-8951-2	Notice of Waiver Of VA Compensation Or Pension To Receive Military Pay And Allowances (2 pages)

Education Forms

22-1919	Conflicting Interests Certification For Proprietary Schools Only (1 page)
22-1990	Application for VA Education Benefits (8 pages). Apply online at VONAPP.
22-1990t	Application and Enrollment Certification For Individualized Tutorial Assistance (38 U.S.C. Chapters 30, 32 or 35 and 10 U.S.C. Chapter 1606) (2 pages)
22-1995	Request For Change of Program or Place of Training (3 pages)
22-1999 series	These forms are available only to school officials with the exception of VAF 22-1999c, which is for correspondence courses. The school must contact their VA Representative to receive forms in this series. A school official can obtain information at the VA Educational Website. Anyone can call toll free 1-888-442-4551 or visit the VA Education Home Page and get answers to their education questions.
22-1999c	Certificate of Affirmation of Enrollment Agreement -Correspondence Course (3 pages)
22-5490	Application For Survivors' and Dependents' Educational Assistance (6 pages)
22-5495	Request for Change of Program or Place of Training Survivors' and Dependents' Educational Assistance (2 pages)

22-6553b-1 Certificate of Lessons Completed (1 page)

22-6553c   Monthly Certification Of Flight Training (2 pages)

22-8690   Time Record (Work-Study Program) (2 pages)

22-8691   Application For Work-Study Allowance (2 pages)

22-8794   Designation of Certifying Official(s) (2 pages)

22-8873   Supplemental Information For Change of Program Or Reenrollment After Unsatisfactory Attendance, Conduct or Progress (2 pages)

22-8889   Application for Educational Assistance Test Program Benefits (2 pages)

Finance Forms

24-0296 1   Direct Deposit Enrollment (1 page)

24-5281   Application For Refund of Education Contributions (VEAP, Chapter 32, Title 38, U.S.C.) (1 page)

Loan Guaranty Forms

26-0285   VA Transmittal List (8 1/2 x 14) (1 page)

26-0286   VA Loan Summary Sheet (8 1/2 x 14) (2 pages)

26-0503   Federal Collection Policy Notice (1 page)

26-0592   Counseling Checklist For Military Homebuyers (1 page)

26-421   Equal Employment Opportunity Certification (2 pages)

26-1802a   HUD/VA Addendum to Uniform Residential Loan Application (5 pages)

26-1805   Request for Determination of Reasonable Value (13 pages)

26-1814   Batch Transmittal - Loan Code Sheet (1 page)

26-1817   Request For Determination Of Loan Guaranty Eligibility - Unremarried Surviving Spouses (1 page)

26-1820   Report And Certification of Loan Disbursement (8 1/2" x 14") (2 pages)

26-1839   Compliance Inspection Report (8 1/2" x 14") (10 pages)

26-1843   Certificate of Reasonable Value (3 pages)

26-1844   Request For Acceptance of Changes In Approved Drawings and Specifications (2 pages - HUD Form 92577)

26-1847   Request For Postponement Of Offsite Or Exterior Onsite Improvements - Home Loan (1 page)

26-1849   Escrow Agreement For Postponed Exterior Onsite Improvements (8 1/2" x 14") (4 pages)

26-1852   Description of Materials (6 pages) (NOTE: This form is the same as the Housing and Urban Development/HUD-92005)

26-1859   Warranty of Completion of Construction (1 page) (NOTE: This form is the same as the Housing and Urban Development/HUD-92544)

26-1880   Request For A Certificate of Eligibility (2 pages) (NOTE: It must be submitted to one of our VA Eligibility Centers, along with acceptable proof of service as described on the instruction page of this form. The instruction sheet does not have to be returned with the completed form.)

26-4555	Veterans Application In Acquiring Specially Adapted Housing or Special Home Adaption Grant (1 page)
26-6378	Escrow Agreement for Postponed Offsite Improvements (4 pages)
26-6381	Application For Assumption Approval and/or Release From Personal Liability to the Government on a Home Loan (1 page)
26-6382	Statement of Purchaser Or Owner Assuming Seller's Loan (2 pages)
26-6393 1	Loan Analysis (8 1/2 x 14) (1 page)
26-6681	Fee or Roster Designation - Application for Fee Personnel Designation (2 pages)
26-6684	Statement of Fee Appraisers or Compliance Inspectors (2 pages)
26-6704	Sales Listing - Loan Guaranty Division (1 page)
26-6705	Offer to Purchase and Contract of Sale (8 1/2 x 14) (2 pages)
26-6705b	Credit Statement of Prospective Purchaser (8 1/2 x 14) (2 pages)
26-6724	Invitation, Bid, and/or Acceptance or Authorization (8 1/2" x 14") (2 pages)
26-6807	Financial Statement (8 1/2 x 14) (2 pages)
26-6850	Notice of Default (2 pages)
26-6850a	Notice of Default and Intention to Foreclose (4 pages)
26-6851	Notice of Intention to Foreclose (1 page)
26-8106	Statement of Veteran Assuming GI Loan (Substitution Entitlement) (1 page)
26-8261a	Request for Certificate of Veteran Status (1 page)
26-8497	Request For Verification of Employment (1 page) (USDA form 410-5)
26-8497a	Request For Verification of Deposit (1 page) (HUD form 92004-F)
26-8599	Manufactured Home Warranty (Limited Warranty) (1 page - 8 1/2" x 14")
26-8630	Manufactured Home Loan Claim Under Loan Guaranty (8 1/2" x 14") (2 pages)
26-8712	Manufactured Home Appraisal Report (1 page)
26-8730	Used Manufactured Home Warranty (Limited Warranty) (1 page)
26-8731a	Water-Plumbing Systems Inspection Report (Manufactured Home) (1 page)
26-8731b	Electrical Systems Inspection Report (Manufactured Home) (1 page)
26-8731c	Fuel and Heating Systems Inspection Report (Manufactured Home) (1 page)
26-8736	Application For Authority To Close Loans On An Automatic Basis – Non-Supervised Lenders (4 pages)
26-8736a	Non-Supervised Lender's Nomination and Recommendation of Credit Underwriter (1 page)
26-8791	VA Affirmative Marketing Certification (2 pages)

26-8812   VA Equal Opportunity Lender Certification (2 pages)

26-8844   Financial Counseling Statement (2 pages) (8 1/2" x 14")

26-8903   Notice of Election To Convey and/or Invoice for Transfer of Property (1 page)

26-8923   Interest Rate Reduction Refinancing Loan Worksheet (1 page)

26-8937   Verification of VA Benefit-Related Indebtedness (1 page)

26-8978   Rights of VA Loan Borrowers (1 page)

Vocational Rehabilitation and Employment Forms

28-1900   Disabled Veterans Application For Vocational Rehabilitation (2 pages) Apply online at VONAPP.

28-1902   Counseling Record - Personal Information (2 pages)

28-1902n   Counseling Record - Narrative Report (Supplemental Sheet) (2 pages)

28-8872   Rehabilitation Plan (2 pages)

28-8872a   Rehabilitation Plan - Continuation Sheet (2 pages)

28-8890   Important Information About Rehabilitation Benefits (2 pages)

Insurance Forms

29-336   Designation of Beneficiary - Government Life Insurance (2 pages)

29-357   Claim for Disability Insurance (3 pages)

29-0563   Veterans Mortgage Life Insurance - Change of Address Statement (1 page)

29-1546   Application For Cash Surrender Value / Application For Policy Loan (2 pages)

29-4125   Claim For One Sum Payment (1 page)

29-4364   Application For Service-Disabled Insurance - (2 pages)

Other Forms Used by VBA

DD 149   Application for Correction of Military Record Under the Provisions of Title 10, U.S. Code, Section 1552 (2 pages) **This form is fillable.**

DD 293 1   Application for the Review of Discharge OR Dismissal From the Armed Forces of the United States (4 pages) **This form is fillable.**

DD 1172   Application for Uniformed Services Identification Card DEERS Enrollment (2 pages)

OF 306   Declaration of Federal Employment (3 pages)

SF 15   Application for 10-Point Veteran's Preference (2 pages)

SF 180   Request Pertaining To Military Records

SGLV 8283 Claim For Death Benefits - Form returned to Office of Servicemembers' Group Life Insurance (2 pages) **This form is fillable.**

SGLV 8285 Request For Insurance - (Servicemembers' Group Life Insurance) (2 pages) **This form is fillable.**

SGLV 8286 Servicemembers' Group Life Insurance Election and Certificate (4 pages) **This form is fillable.**

SGLV 8714 Application For Veterans' Group Life Insurance (5 pages) **This form is fillable.**

VAF 8 Certification of Appeal - (1 page)

VAF 9 Appeal to Board of Veterans' Appeals (5 pages)

VAF 10-10ez Instructions For Completing Application For Health Benefits (4 pages)

VAF 21A Application For Accreditation As A Claims Agent (3 pages) **NEW**

VAF 22A Appointment of Attorney or Agent as Claimant's Representative (1 page)

VAF 3288 Request For And Consent To Release of Information From Claimant's Records (2 pages)

VAF 4107 Your Rights to Appeal Our Decision (2 pages)

VAF 4107a Your Right to Appeal Our Decision (2 pages)

VAF 4107b Notice of Procedural And Appellate Rights (1 page) (Spanish Version)

VAF 5655 Financial Status Report (2 pages)

40-1330 Application for Standard Government Headstone or Marker for Installation in a Private or State Veterans' Cemetery (5 pages)

Applying Online with VONAPP

The VONAPP (Veterans On Line Applications) Web site is an official U.S. Department of Veterans Affairs (VA) Web site designed so that individuals can apply for benefits through the Internet. This is a first step toward an electronic VA. VONAPP allows veterans electronic access to file applications with the VA online.

U.S. military veterans and some servicemembers within six months of separation or retirement can apply for compensation, pension, and vocational rehabilitation benefits using VONAPP. U.S. military veterans, service members with two years of service, and members of the Selected Reserve can apply for education benefits.

How Is Using This Site Different from Visiting a VA Office?

When you use this site to complete and send an application to VA, your application will be sent directly to the VA office with jurisdiction over your application. Processing will begin right away, and you will receive a response from the VA office letting you know the status of your application.

If you use the VA Form 21-526, you will be using a special form with a design based on the results of research in readability and the use of plain English. VA has a major initiative to rewrite letters and redesign forms based on plain English called Reader-Focused Writing.

VA Forms Now Available in VONAPP

- VA Form 21-526, Veteran's Application for Compensation and/or Pension

- VA Form 28-1900, Disabled Veterans Application for Vocational Rehabilitation
- VA Form 22-1990, Application for Education Benefits

What "Helps" Are on This Site?

Home Page Buttons: We have designed this site so that you can have help features and background information at all times. The VONAPP Home Page has buttons to provide in-depth information for specific topics:

- What do I need to run VONAPP on my computer?

- VA Partners - Service Organizations

- Instructions for Filling Out Applications

- Frequently Asked Questions (FAQs)

- Who should use VONAPP

- State and County Organizations and Other Help

Bonus Section: Veterans' Preference

The Office of Personnel Management (OPM) administers entitlement to veterans' *preference* in employment under title 5, United States Code, and oversees other statutory employment requirements in titles 5 and 38. (Title 38 also governs veterans' entitlement to *benefits* administered by the Department of Veterans Affairs (VA).)

Both title 5 and title 38 use many of the same terms, but in different ways. For example, service during a "war" is used to determine entitlement to veterans' preference and service credit under title 5. OPM has always interpreted this to mean **a war declared by Congress**. But title 38 defines "period of war" to include many non-declared wars, including Korea, Vietnam, and the Persian Gulf. Such conflicts entitle a veteran to VA **benefits** under title 38, but not necessarily to **preference or service credit** under title 5. Thus it is critically important to use the correct definitions in determining eligibility for specific rights and benefits in employment.

Why Preference Is Given

Since the time of the Civil War, veterans of the Armed Forces have been given some degree of preference in appointments to Federal jobs. Recognizing their sacrifice, Congress enacted laws to prevent veterans seeking Federal employment from being penalized for their time in military service. Veterans' preference recognizes the economic loss suffered by citizens who have served their country in uniform, restores veterans to a favorable competitive position for Government employment, and acknowledges the larger obligation owed to disabled veterans.

Veterans' preference in its present form comes from the Veterans' Preference Act of 1944, as amended, and is now codified in various provisions of title 5, United States Code. By law, veterans who are disabled or who served on active duty in the Armed Forces during certain specified time periods or in military campaigns are entitled to preference over others in hiring from competitive lists of eligibles and also in retention during reductions in force.

In addition to receiving preference in **competitive** appointments, veterans may be considered for special **noncompetitive** appointments for which only they are eligible.

When Preference Applies

Preference in hiring applies to permanent and temporary positions in the competitive and excepted services of the executive branch. Preference does not apply to positions in the Senior Executive Service or to executive branch positions for which Senate confirmation is required. The legislative and judicial branches of the Federal Government also are exempt from the Veterans' Preference Act **unless** the positions are in the competitive service (Government Printing Office, for example) or have been made subject to the Act by another law.

Preference applies in hiring from civil service examinations conducted by the Office of Personnel Management (OPM) and agencies under delegated examining authority, for most excepted service jobs including Veterans' Readjustment

Appointments (VRA), and when agencies make temporary, term, and overseas limited appointments. Veterans' preference does not apply to promotion, reassignment, change to lower grade, transfer or reinstatement.

Veterans' preference does not require an agency to use any particular appointment process. Agencies have broad authority under law to hire from any appropriate source of eligibles including special appointing authorities. An agency may consider candidates already in the civil service from an agency-developed merit promotion list or it may reassign a current employee, transfer an employee from another agency, or reinstate a former Federal employee. In addition, agencies are required to give priority to displaced employees before using civil service examinations and similar hiring methods.

Civil service examination: Title 5 United States Code (U.S.C.) 3304-3330, title 5 Code of Federal Regulations (CFR) Part 332, OPM Delegation Agreements with individual agencies, OPM Examining Handbook, OPM Delegated Examining Operations Handbook; *Excepted service appointments, including VRA's*: 5 U.S.C. 3320; 5 CFR Part 302; *Temporary and term employment:* 5 CFR Parts 316 and 333; *Overseas limited employment:* 5 CFR Part 301; *Career Transition Program:* 5 CFR Part 330, Subparts F and G.

Types of Preference

To receive preference, a veteran must have been **separated from active duty in the Armed Forces with an honorable or general discharge**. As defined in 5 U.S.C. 2101(2), "Armed Forces" means the Army, Navy, Air Force, Marine Corps and Coast Guard. The veteran must also be eligible under one of the preference categories below (also shown on the Standard Form (SF) 50, *Notification of Personnel Action*).

Military retirees at the rank of major, lieutenant commander, or higher are not eligible for preference in appointment unless they are disabled veterans. (This does not apply to Reservists who will not begin drawing military retired pay until age 60.)

Active duty for training or inactive duty by National Guard or Reserve soldiers does not qualify as "active duty" for preference.

For purposes of this chapter and 5 U.S.C. 2108, "war" means only those armed conflicts declared by Congress as war and includes World War II, which covers the period from December 7, 1941, to April 28, 1952.

When applying for Federal jobs, eligible veterans should claim preference on their application or resume. Applicants claiming 10-point preference must complete Standard Form (SF) 15, *Application for 10-Point Veteran Preference*, and submit the requested documentation.

The following preference categories and points are based on 5 U.S.C. 2108 and 3309 as modified by a length of service requirement in 38 U.S.C. 5303A(d). (The letters following each category, e.g., "TP," are a shorthand reference used by OPM in competitive examinations.)

5-Point Preference (TP)

Five points are added to the **passing** examination score or rating of a veteran who served:

- During a war; **or**
- During the period April 28, 1952 through July 1, 1955; **or**
- For more than 180 consecutive days, other than for training, any part of which occurred after January 31, 1955, and before October 15, 1976; **or**
- During the Gulf War from August 2, 1990, through January 2, 1992; **or**
- In a campaign or expedition for which a campaign medal has been authorized. Any Armed Forces Expeditionary medal or campaign badge, including El Salvador, Lebanon, Grenada, Panama, Southwest Asia, Somalia, and Haiti, qualifies for preference.

A campaign medal holder or Gulf War veteran who originally enlisted after September 7, 1980, (or began active duty on or after October 14, 1982, and has not previously completed 24 months of continuous active duty) must have served continuously for 24 months or the full period called or ordered to active duty. The 24-month service requirement does not apply to 10-point preference eligibles separated for disability incurred or aggravated in the line of duty, or to veterans separated for hardship or other reasons under 10 U.S.C. 1171 or 1173.

10-Point Compensable Disability Preference (CP)

Ten points are added to the **passing** examination score or rating of:

- A veteran who served at any time **and** who has a compensable service-connected disability rating of at least 10 percent but less than 30 percent.

10-Point 30 Percent Compensable Disability Preference (CPS)

Ten points are added to the **passing** examination score or rating of a veteran who served at any time and who has a compensable service-connected disability rating of 30 percent or more.

10-Point Disability Preference (XP)

Ten points are added to the **passing** examination score or rating of:

- A veteran who served at any time and has a present service-connected disability or is receiving compensation, disability retirement benefits, or pension from the military or the Department of Veterans Affairs but does not qualify as a CP or CPS; **or**
- A veteran who received a Purple Heart.

10-Point Derived Preference (XP)

Ten points are added to the **passing** examination score or rating of spouses, widows, widowers, or mothers of veterans as described below. This type of preference is usually referred to as "derived preference" because it is based on service of a veteran who is not able to use the preference.

Both a mother and a spouse (including widow or widower) may be entitled to preference on the basis of the same veteran's service if they both meet the requirements. However, neither may receive preference if the veteran is living **and** is qualified for Federal employment.

Spouse

Ten points are added to the **passing** examination score or rating of the spouse of a disabled veteran who is disqualified for a Federal position along the general lines of his or her usual occupation **because of a service-connected disability**. Such a disqualification may be presumed **when the veteran is unemployed and**

- is rated by appropriate military or Department of Veterans Affairs authorities to be 100 percent disabled and/or unemployable; **or**
- has retired, been separated, or resigned from a civil service position on the basis of a disability that is service-connected in origin; **or**
- has attempted to obtain a civil service position or other position along the lines of his or her usual occupation and has failed to qualify **because of a service-connected disability**.

Preference may be allowed in other circumstances but anything less than the above warrants a more careful analysis.

NOTE: Veterans' preference for spouses is different than the preference the Department of Defense is required by law to extend to spouses of active duty members in filling its civilian positions. For more information on that program, contact the Department of Defense.

Widow/Widower

Ten points are added to the passing examination score or rating of the widow or widower of a veteran who was not divorced from the veteran, has not remarried, or the remarriage was annulled, and the veteran either:

- served during a war or during the period April 28, 1952, through July 1, 1955, or in a campaign or expedition for which a campaign medal has been authorized; **or**
- died while on active duty that included service described immediately above under conditions that would not have been the basis for other than an honorable or general discharge.

Mother of a Deceased Veteran

Ten points are added to the **passing** examination score or rating of the mother of a veteran who died under honorable conditions while on active duty during a war or during the period April 28, 1952, through July 1, 1955, or in a campaign or expedition for which a campaign medal has been authorized; **and**

- she is or was married to the father of the veteran; **and**
- she lives with her totally and permanently disabled husband (either the veteran's father or her husband through remarriage); **or**

- she is widowed, divorced, or separated from the veteran's father and has not remarried; **or**
- she remarried but is widowed, divorced, or legally separated from her husband when she claims preference.

Mother of a Disabled Veteran

Ten points are added to the **passing** examination score or rating of a mother of a living disabled veteran if the veteran was separated with an honorable or general discharge from active duty performed at any time **and** is permanently and totally disabled from a service-connected injury or illness; and the mother:

- is or was married to the father of the veteran; **and**
- lives with her totally and permanently disabled husband (either the veteran's father or her husband through remarriage); **or**
- is widowed, divorced, or separated from the veteran's father and has not remarried; **or**
- remarried but is widowed, divorced, or legally separated from her husband when she claims preference.

Note: Preference is not given to widows or mothers of deceased veterans who qualify for preference under 5 U.S.C. 2108 (1) (B), (C) or (2). Thus, the widow or mother of a deceased disabled veteran who served after 1955, but did not serve in a war, campaign, or expedition, would not be entitled to preference.

5 U.S.C. 2108 and 3309; 38 U.S.C. 5303A

Index